Beginning the Journey
Your First 30 Days as a Christ-Follower

By Gene Roncone

All scripture notations are taken from The Holy Bible, New International Version®, NIV®, Copyright© 1973, 1978, 1984, 2011 by Biblica, Inc., unless otherwise noted.

ABOUT THE AUTHOR

Gene Roncone has a passion to see people discover a life-giving relationship with Jesus Christ. He came to Christ at the age of 15 from a life of drugs and alcohol. His life has been transformed by the power of God, and he now loves helping new believers get a firm start in their spiritual journey. Gene presently leads the Rocky Mountain Ministry Network where he provides support, resourcing, and training for nearly 170 churches and 600 ministers serving over 44,000 constituents in Colorado and Utah. He enjoys reading and writing in the Colorado wilderness and spending time with his wife, Rhonda, and their adult children and their grandchildren. You can contact Gene through www.generoncone.org.

Dedicated to Albert and Margaret Yanno. As a new believer, they discipled me in the early days and months of my faith. Their grace could handle seeing me at my worst because their faith could imagine me at my best.

Table of Contents

Introduction

Congratulations! You have recently decided to follow Christ and place Him at the center of your life. Whether your decision was made in a church's worship service, a small group Bible study, or in the privacy of your own heart, I want to help you get a solid start on your new journey.

That is why I created this resource to coach you through the first 30 days of your new decision. All you need to do is read each day's topic and a corresponding portion of the Bible every day. Those two things will only take you about 20-25 minutes a day.

It is my prayer that this resource will help to continue the new and exciting things God is doing in your life. At the end of each day's reading, I have provided a few reflection questions that will help you process the topic. These questions are designed to get you thinking and to help you apply the lessons learned. You can either go through them on your own, use them as a guide for one-on-one conversations with a mature believer, or in a small group that uses this book as a group study. You can also use the audio version found at www.gojourney.org.

I know what you might be thinking. "Why should I work through this resource? I'm busy. I've got a night class, three kids, and homework", or "I've got a demanding job". I can promise you that many of your questions will be answered,

and you will grow in your understanding of God and the Bible.

The reading plan is a simple schedule that will help you work your way through the Bible. If you do not have a Bible, just email your pastor and request one. I feel certain the church will be glad to get you one.

It is important for you to give the seed of faith time and opportunity to grow. In the meantime, I am here to help so let's get started with Day 1.

Day 1: Hardwired for Eternity

Congratulations on your recent decision to become a Christ-follower. You just did something that will forever change your past, present, and future. You decided to place Christ at the center of your heart and fulfill His eternal purpose for your life. Let me explain.

Most of us have used some kind of GPS navigational device. These systems have an internal beacon that is in constant communication with satellites orbiting the earth. In very much the same way, God has hardwired a spiritual beacon into your soul. It is always calling, yearning, and nudging us to stay connected to our eternal maker.

What is this beacon? The Bible says it is eternity, and God has hardwired it into our hearts. That is what the Bible means when it says: "He has also set eternity in the human heart" (Ecclesiastes 3:11). When you decided to follow Christ, you responded to the eternal beacon God placed in your soul.

You see, you were hardwired with an eternal design. God created you differently than any of His creations! Genesis 1:26 tells us that "God said, 'Let us make mankind in our image, in our likeness.'" Genesis 2:7 says that "the LORD God formed a man from the dust of the ground and breathed into his nostrils the breath of life, and the man became a living being."

A friend of mine who works in a DNA lab told me that one way a scientist can collect DNA is to have a person simply blow up a balloon. Your DNA is in the water molecules of your breath which becomes trapped inside the balloon. Something like that happened when God breathed life into humanity. A piece of God's eternal nature is deep inside each of us. We will always be a reflection of God because we have eternal DNA!

You were also hardwired with an eternal desire. That is what the Bible means when it says that "He has also set eternity in the human heart" (Ecclesiastes 3:11). God has placed within the heart of every person a desire to experience the eternal. That is why there was something inside of you that:

- Desires to be reconciled with God.
- Longs to understand your purpose in life.
- Cannot be satisfied with the temporary things of this world.

We have eternal DNA in our spirits. That is why nothing in our present life on earth can totally satisfy us and why we are forever wrestling until we answer the eternal beacon. Do you know what dissatisfaction is? It is the result of an eternal soul's trying to find fulfillment in temporary things. One of my favorite authors, C. S. Lewis, put it this way: "If we find ourselves with a desire that nothing in this world can satisfy, the most probable explanation is that we were made for another world" (*Mere Christianity*). I love that!

You have also been hardwired with an eternal destiny. Okay, hold on to your seat because this is about to get interesting. Your body will die, but your soul is going to live forever! Why? Because God has breathed eternity into your

heart. Your existence is not like a disposable cup. God has created you with a soul, and that means death IS NOT the end of your existence. You have an eternal component that will live forever. Where that forever is depends on the choices you make while living in your body on earth. You will either live forever with God or forever separated from Him. The Bible tells us that "people are destined to die once, and after that to face judgment" (Hebrews 9:27).

Jesus also spoke about a day when every person will stand before God. Those who are not reconciled to God through Christ will face the consequences for rejecting Him. Jesus described this: "These will go away into eternal punishment, but the righteous into eternal life" (Matthew 25:46 NASB). That about wraps up our eternal accommodations. It is either eternal life or eternal separation from God.

That is what is so exciting about your decision to follow Christ! God created each of us in His image. With that, He gave us the power to choose. Think about that. God loved us so much that He let us choose...even if that choice is to reject Him, but you used the power of choice to make things right with God through Christ. As a spiritual being created in God's image, you have embraced His eternal plan for your life.

So stay on the journey and be sure to read your Bible. As a matter of fact, I would like to encourage you to read three chapters a day. Don't worry though; chapters in the Bible are much shorter than chapters in a book. The reading for today is John 1-3 and will only take about 15 minutes to complete. These chapters talk about the decision you have made and how you have experienced this new spiritual birth.

It is also important to keep reading this book so we can journey through your first month together. Do you find yourself wondering just what happened to you since your decision? If so, that's good because tomorrow we will talk about what happened in the spiritual realm when you made your decision to follow Christ.

Day 1 Reflection Questions

- Before you decided to follow Jesus, did you ever find yourself thinking about life after death? Has this decision changed the way you think about it now?
- How does knowing that God breathed life into humanity impact the way you view your own existence?
- Why do we not find lasting satisfaction in temporary things, such as exciting experiences, nice possessions, or important achievements?
- Jesus is the only way to an eternity spent with God. What are some of the things that have proven themselves incapable of giving you eternal purpose? Perhaps a career, a reputation, or a hobby?
- In today's reading, you came across one of the most famous statements in the Bible: "For God so loved the world that he gave his one and only Son, that whoever believes in him shall not perish but have eternal life. For God did not send his Son into the world to condemn the world, but to save the world through him" (John 3:16-17). As you read that, what words or phrases caught your attention, and why?

Day 2: What Just Happened?

You recently decided to become a Christian. This step is the most important decision you will ever make in your life. You may have all sorts of thoughts, emotions, and questions. Some feel joy, relief, wonder, anxiety, enthusiasm, and freedom. Others feel no emotions at all, but that's okay because we are all different.

Now that you have made that decision, I want to talk to you about three things that have happened to you in a spiritual sense.

- You have experienced the salvation of Christ.
- You have received God's forgiveness.
- You have found God's acceptance.

Let me briefly share about each of these experiences.

First, you experienced the salvation of Christ. When Christians refer to "being saved," they mean that Jesus has rescued them from the consequences of a life and eternity without God. Before becoming a Christ-follower, you existed in a state of spiritual death; but now you have been rescued by God's love, forgiveness, and acceptance.

Before I was a Christian, I had a hard time believing I was worthy of God's love; but the Bible helped me better understand spiritual things. John 3:16 says, "For God so loved the world that he gave his one and only Son, that whoever believes in him shall not perish but have eternal life."

Before becoming a Christian, you exercised your freedom of choice not to choose God; but that could not stop God from loving you. God loved you so much that He sent Jesus to this world to provide a personal opportunity for you to choose eternal life. No matter what you have done and no matter what you might do in the future, God loves you.

Second, you received God's forgiveness. Knowing that the consequences of our sin is a debt we cannot possibly pay, God decided to pay it for us. Our sin wrote a check that our spiritual bank account of goodness could not cover. That is why Jesus died on the cross for your sins. When you became a Christian, you probably told God about the sins you have committed and asked for His forgiveness. And you know what? God forgave you! That is why the Bible says that "if we confess our sins, he is faithful and just and will forgive us our sins and purify us from all unrighteousness" (1 John 1:9). The Contemporary English Version (CEV) of the Bible puts it this way: "If we confess our sins to God, he can always be trusted to forgive us and take our sins away."

You might also be wondering, "But how will I deal with my future sins?" The same forgiveness continues to be available. The sacrifice that Jesus made over two thousand years ago was so pure and holy that it has the power to forgive past, present, and future sins. That is what the Bible means when it says that Jesus "has appeared once for all at the culmination of the ages to do away with sin by the sacrifice of himself" (Hebrews 9:26). Now you can see why choosing to follow Christ is so important. As you confess your sins to God, He will forgive you—again and again!

Third, you are experiencing God's acceptance. You and I live in a world where most things are conditional. We get things by working either to deserve or become worthy of receiving them, but the amazing thing about God is that He created you and loves you no matter what you do or where you have been. You do not have to do something good to earn His acceptance. He accepts you just as you are.

This is what the Bible calls "grace": God's undeserved or unearned favor. It is God personally absorbing the consequences we would have otherwise received without Him. One of my favorite verses in the Bible explains what happened to you when you became a Christian. "For it is by grace you have been saved, through faith—and this is not from yourselves, it is the gift of God—not by works, so that no one can boast" (Ephesians 2:8-9).

God is your Father who accepts you just as you are. He loves you; and as you grow, He will help you to become more and more like He is. He does not accept you on the basis of your being able to avoid sin; He accepts you because He has loved you, saved you, and forgiven you.

If someone asks you what happened to you, just tell them you found God's love, forgiveness, and acceptance; and you have not regretted it.

Today's reading is John 4-6. These three chapters talk about people who experienced God's grace the same way you have. They speak about the Samaritan woman, an official's son, and a lame man who were all healed along with thousands who were miraculously fed by Jesus. Like you, they all experienced the grace and forgiveness of God. Reading God's

Word will be one of the most life-giving things you do all day so don't neglect it.

Tomorrow we will talk about how to know if the decision you made to follow Christ was real or not. Until then, continue the journey.

Day 2 Reflection Questions

- What thoughts and feelings have you had since deciding to follow Jesus?
- How does it feel to know that Jesus came with the purpose of rescuing you from sinfulness and spiritual death?
- First John 1:9 says that "if we confess our sins, he is faithful and just and will forgive us our sins and purify us from all unrighteousness." What does this verse tell you about God's character and the way He is working in your life?
- Why do we sometimes find it so hard to believe that God, our loving Father, accepts us with open arms?
- In today's reading, you saw Jesus serve and interact with many different people. Did any of these stories remind you of your own encounter with Jesus? If so, how?

Day 3: Reassurance Insurance

Welcome to Day 3 of your new life! Today your Bible reading is John 7-9. These three chapters tell about who Jesus is and why we can believe Him. Have you read it yet? If not, don't forget. God's Word is like food for your spirit.

How are you feeling about this new decision? It can be exciting and sobering at the same time. Believe me, I know.

I remember buying my first home. I knew it was the right decision; and the closer it came to the closing, the more excited my wife and I became. We signed the papers and waited for final approval, but something happened two days later. I started thinking about how big this decision was and the risk involved. I called my realtor and suggested that I might need more time to think it through. She calmly told us to relax and affirmed that we had made a good decision. She told me that the apprehension I was feeling was common and was called "buyer's remorse." Buyer's remorse is the feeling of doubt that often follows big decisions. It is common for people to experience it after they choose a college, commit to a career, buy a car, or purchase their first home.

It is natural to doubt or "second guess" big decisions. I think the same thing is true when it comes to spiritual decisions. We wonder if what happened was real. We wonder if we will be truly committed and carry it out. We wonder if our decision was based on fact, feelings, or momentary emotions. If you think about it, however, those concerns only confirm that we are taking God seriously and want to be true to our commitment to follow Him.

There are four things that helped me when I faced these very same questions.

First, you know you are saved because the Bible is true. Your decision was not based on something you created or invented. Your decision was based on something the Bible promised—salvation for those who recognize their sin and confess their need for God. Following are a few Scriptures that make this promise.

> John 3:16: "For God so loved the world that he gave his one and only Son, that whoever believes in him shall not perish but have eternal life."

> 1 John 1:9: "If we confess our sins, he is faithful and just and will forgive us our sins and purify us from all unrighteousness."

> Ephesians 2:8-9: "For it is by grace you have been saved, through faith—and this not from yourselves, it is the gift of God—not by works, so that no one can boast."

Second, you know you are saved because God has not changed. God has not changed since you made your decision to follow Him. He still loves you! He still reaches out and still calls you to His eternal plan for your life. That is why God reassures us about His own consistency when He says: "I the LORD do not change" (Malachi 3:6).

Third, you know you are saved because it is not about your accomplishments. Our confidence in salvation is not based on our own goodness, worthiness, or ability to do good things. That is why the Bible says that our salvation is "not by works of righteousness which we have done, but according to his mercy he saved us" (Titus 3:5 KJV).

Fourth, you know you are saved because your heart wants to please God. The Bible tells us that God's children have a yearning inside of them to please and obey Him. That is what the Apostle Paul means when he says: "You have not received a spirit that makes you fearful slaves. Instead, you received God's Spirit when he adopted you as his own children. Now we call him, 'Abba, Father.' For his Spirit joins with our spirit to affirm that we are God's children" (Romans 8:15-16 NLT).

The very fact that you are concerned about your own spiritual state is evidence that God has done a miracle in your life. Your newly changed behavior, hunger for God's Word, and desire for spiritual growth are all evidence that you are NOW a child of God.

Doubt wants to rob us by reframing facts, but the facts have not changed. God still promises salvation and has provided for that salvation by giving His one and only Son. Your confidence is not in yourself or dependent upon feelings, circumstances, or the environment of your decision. Your confidence is in something more certain than you can ever imagine—the promise of a never-changing God. That is what the Bible calls faith!

Don't forget to read today's three chapters. We'll talk more tomorrow.

Day 3 Reflection Questions

- What kind of doubts have you had since committing to Jesus? How did today's chapters help you address those?
- An early Christian named Paul said, "All Scripture is God-breathed" (2 Timothy 3:16). How does knowing that the Bible is the inspired Word of God give you confidence in what you read?
- Why is it important to remember that your salvation has nothing to do with your own good works? Do you find that confusing, relieving, or encouraging? Anything else?
- How has God changed your heart in the last few days?
- What are some things that Jesus says about himself in today's reading (John 7-9)?

Day 4: Why Did Jesus Have to Die?

This is Day 4 of your new journey, and today's Bible reading is John 10-12. In these three chapters, Jesus speaks several times about His life's mission and why He came to earth to die for our sins. If you have taken the time to read these important chapters, you know how powerful they are.

I remember when I decided to become a Christ-follower. I saw a slideshow depicting the crucifixion of Christ and was blown away by His love for me. The love of God was irresistible, and I remember wondering why Jesus had to die for my sins. I was so unworthy, and it all seemed so unfair. You might be asking the same question.

However, before we answer the question, "Why did Jesus have to die?" it is important to understand that Jesus saw His own death as necessary. He clearly understood that His mission on earth involved laying down His life as a sacrifice for mankind. "Then Jesus began to tell them that the Son of Man, must suffer many terrible things and be rejected by the elders, the leading priests, and the teachers of religious law. He would be killed, but three days later he would rise from the dead" (Mark 8:31 NLT).

So why did Jesus have to die? Perhaps a better question might be—why was Jesus willing to die? Let me give you four simple reasons.

The first reason Jesus had to die is because God could not ignore sin at the expense of His own character. The Bible tells us that God is totally and 100 percent holy. If God were to ignore sin or pretend it did not happen, He would be untrue to himself. If you discovered your child stole money from your neighbor, the fact that your child might apologize or that you would forgive them is not enough. Your integrity would require you to own what happened, return the money, and ask for your neighbor's forgiveness. In very much the same way, God refused to compromise His character by tolerating or ignoring our sin. Consequently, Jesus became the only worthy sacrifice to redeem those affected by its impact. God is all merciful, all powerful, and all forgiving. God is also holy, righteous, just, and the only one worthy enough to pay the debt for our sins. His own integrity required it.

The second reason Jesus had to die is because sin separates us from God. When I first became a Christian, I had a hard time understanding how Adam's sin in the Garden of Eden made me a sinner also. Before I talk about what the Bible says about this subject, let me use an illustration. As a child, I never decided or chose to become a United States citizen. I inherited citizenship by virtue of the fact that my parents were U.S. citizens. Like it or not, my legal status has nothing to do with a decision I ever made or did not make. It is my "U.S.A. nature." In the same way that we are born into a secular state, we are also born into a spiritual state. Unfortunately, none of us are born as citizens of heaven; we have to emigrate, and Jesus's death gives us the passport.

In a spiritual sense, sin entered the world through one man's disobedience (Adam's), and now all of us as human descendants are born into this "sin nature." That is also what the

Bible means when it says that "when Adam sinned, sin entered the world. Adam's sin brought death, so death spread to everyone, for everyone sinned" (Romans 5:12 NLT). The Bible also affirms this in other verses: "For everyone has sinned; we all fall short of God's glorious standard" (Romans 3:23 NLT), and "your iniquities have separated you from your God; your sins have hidden his face from you, so that he will not hear" (Isaiah 59:2).

The third reason Jesus had to die is to counteract the consequence of eternal separation from God. The Bible teaches us that sin's punishment is eternal death and separation from God. "The wages of sin is death, but the free gift of God is eternal life through Christ Jesus our Lord" (Romans 6:23 NLT). But God volunteered to intervene on our behalf! That is what the Bible means when it says that "just as sin ruled over all people and brought them to death, now God's wonderful grace rules instead, giving us right standing with God and resulting in eternal life through Jesus Christ our Lord" (Romans 5:21 NLT).

The fourth reason Jesus had to die is because He is the only one pure enough to serve as a substitute for our sin. Our own sacrifice, no matter how extreme, is not sufficient to compensate for sin. Why? Because paying the price for our sin required something perfect, something totally pure, and something without fault.

It would make no sense for a lawyer to say to a judge, "Look, Your Honor, instead of putting my admittedly guilty client in jail, how about you put this other person in jail instead?" That would be crazy, unfair, and unjust. But imagine if the lawyer said, "Your Honor, I have never committed a single crime in my entire life; however, I propose you send me to jail in my client's place." Jesus's sacrifice is not only that outrageous but also even more amazing! It is as though the guiltless judge himself stepped down off the bench and said, "I, myself, will pay the penalty and serve the sentence for your crime. Go. You are pardoned."

That is why the Bible refers to Jesus as the perfect ransom. When we were being held hostage to sin, God sent Him as the pure, complete, and everlasting sacrifice to make eternal payment for our sin. That is what the Bible means when it says, "For you know that God paid a ransom to save you from the empty life you inherited from your ancestors. And it was not paid with mere gold or silver, which lose their value. It was the precious blood of Christ, the sinless, spotless Lamb of God" (1 Peter 1:18-19 NLT).

All through the Bible, the Scriptures teach us that Christ is the only way to experience eternal life. Peter said: "Salvation is found in no one else, for there is no other name under heaven given to mankind by which we must be saved" (Acts 4:12). Peter later would claim that the Old Testament prophets foretold these things: "All the prophets testify about him that everyone who believes in him receives forgiveness of sins through his name" (Acts 10:43). Jesus himself claimed to be God's exclusive path to salvation: "I am the way and the truth and the life. No one comes to the Father except through me" (John 14:6). The Apostle Paul said: "For there is one God and one mediator between God and mankind, the man Christ Jesus, who gave himself as a ransom for all people" (1 Timothy 2:5-6). God himself told Joseph: "You are to give him the name Jesus, because he will save his people from their sins" (Matthew 1:21).

The exclusivity of Jesus as God's conduit of salvation is clearly mentioned in Scripture and taught by the prophets, the apostles, Jesus himself, and God the Father.

However, is it fair for God to insist that Christ is the only way to eternal life? If God is perfect and just, then He must also be truthful; and if He is truthful, He can be believed and is incapable of lying. Therefore, when God's Word tells us there is one way to salvation through the death and resurrection of His Son Jesus Christ, we have only two logical options: to believe God is true or to doubt His character and honesty.

As much as we may want to believe there may be other options for salvation, there are not. The Bible tells us that God already offered us His best and only solution: "God made him who had no sin to be sin for us, so that in him we might become the righteousness of God" (2 Corinthians 5:21). In other words, Jesus voluntarily accepted the responsibility for our sins and absorbed the punishment, consequences, and shame associated with our spiritual rebellion on the cross. He saved us by doing for us what we could not do for ourselves.

God did not just save us FROM something; He also saved us FOR something. That something is called spiritual growth, and we will be talking about it tomorrow. Until then, keep reading those three chapters.

Day 4 Reflection Questions

- Why did Jesus have to die for our sins? And why was He willing to do so?

- What does it mean to say that God is "holy" and "just"?
- Since Jesus is God in the flesh, we can affirm that He is holy and just. How does that make His sacrifice so amazing—even "outrageous"?
- Was there anything in today's chapters that left you scratching your head? Who can you talk to in order to get some clarity?
- Based on today's reading (John 10-12), how would you summarize Jesus's life's mission?

Day 5: How to Grow Spiritually

This is Day 5 of your journey, and today's Bible reading is John 13-15.

In Chapter 15, Jesus compared our spiritual lives to a vine that needs to grow and bear fruit. I like that analogy because life is stressful and can drain your spirit; but God's Word is a life-giving catalyst that will pour energy back into you. Don't neglect it; it is a worthy investment.

Do you know what the word "Christian" originally meant? It referred to people who identified themselves with Christ's teaching and lifestyle. In other words, they had become reflections of "Christ" or Christ "mini-me's." Okay, so the Austin Powers image might not be the best, but you get the picture. We are talking about someone who was a serious student of Jesus. In biblical times, this was called being a disciple.

The word "disciple" means "learner." It refers to those who had left their former way of life to follow Jesus and learn from Him. That is what you are...a Christ-follower, a believer, and a disciple.

Being a disciple does not mean you must quit your job and check into a monastery. God wants you to live life to the fullest and grow in your faith, but how do you nurture this new relationship with God so that it grows stronger rather than weaker? I want to answer that question by addressing four ways to keep growing in your faith. Each one is a necessary ingredient to growth. They are worship, Bible reading, serving, and loving others.

The first ingredient of spiritual growth is experiencing God in worship. Soon after a person becomes a follower of Christ, the Bible encourages them to start identifying with a community of faith in public worship. Christianity is not an independent study which is why the first followers of Christ were committed to community and worshiping together. The first step to growing is being faithful to weekly church services and worshiping with other believers. That is why I would like you to make church attendance a priority in your life. Start by setting a goal to be at no less than three out of four Sunday worship services a month. Did you get that? That is three out of four Sundays a month. Going to church is like going to the gas station. It replenishes the spiritual fuel that gets used up in the daily grind of life.

The second ingredient of healthy growth is learning more about God's Word and how to apply it to your life. Learning and living God's Word is what the Bible calls "discipleship." It is studying the teachings of Jesus and applying them to life. Peter stresses the importance of God's Word for spiritual growth: "Like newborn babies, crave pure spiritual milk, so that by it you may grow up in your salvation" (1 Peter 2:2). This is why I am giving you a simple daily reading plan. It will help you get a solid start in your new journey. After we finish this journey, I am going to ask you to continue reading God's Word and attend a Bible study at a church in your community. These Bible studies are like book clubs except the book is the Bible. I am part of one, and it is the highlight of my week.

The third ingredient of spiritual growth is serving God and others. Each and every one of us were created with a unique mix of spiritual gifts, passions, abilities, temperament, and experiences that complement where God wants us to serve. We need to identify and develop our God-given gifts and use them in service to God and others. This service can take place in your local church, community, or nonprofit organization that helps the underserved. It is important to remember that you are not an island unto yourselves. You need others, and they need you!

The fourth ingredient of healthy growth is loving our world. You are part of God's plan to reach others. God wants to use you to bring hope and healing to those around you. Beginning in your own circle of relationships and extending beyond your city and to the farthest parts of the planet, God wants you to share His love with others. Jesus called us to be world-changers when He said, "You will be my witnesses in Jerusalem, and in all Judea and Samaria, and to the ends of the earth" (Acts 1:8). This aspect of spiritual growth is so critical that it was very last commandment Jesus gave His followers: "Go and make disciples of all nations, baptizing them in the name of the Father and of the Son and of the Holy Spirit, and teaching them to obey everything I have commanded you" (Matthew 28:19-20). It is part of His eternal purpose, and we are not really happy or fulfilled unless we are part of it.

Worship, God's Word, serving, and loving are all essential ingredients to spiritual growth. If only one ingredient is missing, our growth is stalled and can become strained. Right now, start with worship and Bible reading; and the rest will come more easily.

Tomorrow we will talk more about why the Bible is so important. Until then, continue the journey and take those 15 minutes to read John 13-15.

Day 5 Reflection Questions

- What does the word "disciple" mean and how does that title describe your new life in Christ?
- Why is it so important to worship God with other believers in your local church?
- Practically speaking, what steps can you take to consistently act upon the things you read about in the Bible?
- Have you ever thought about using your gifts to serve others and share your faith? Does that idea excite you or intimidate you? Why?
- Jesus told His followers, "Remain in me, as I also remain in you. No branch can bear fruit by itself; it must remain in the vine. Neither can you bear fruit unless you remain in me" (John 15:4). According to this command, what do growth and productivity depend on?

Day 6: Why the Bible Is Important

It is Day 6 of your new journey, and today's Bible reading is John 16-18.

In Chapter 16, Jesus promised the disciples that after He returned to heaven, He would send the Holy Spirit to guide them in truth. Isn't it amazing to think that God's Holy Spirit is guiding you as you read His Word? That is why I want to talk to you today about the most important ingredient in your spiritual growth and health: daily Bible reading.

As you have probably recognized, the Bible is not just another book but the most important, clear, and powerful way God has revealed himself to us. It says that "all Scripture is inspired by God and is useful to teach us what is true and to make us realize what is wrong in our lives" (2 Timothy 3:16 NLT).

The word "inspired" in this scripture literally means "God-breathed." When we say the Bible is inspired, we mean that the Holy Spirit miraculously worked through each biblical writer during the 1,500-year span of time that the Scriptures were written. As we understand what each writer meant to say in their own time and context, we discover transformational truth for our own lives and culture.

The Bible teaches us in many ways. Sometimes we learn from the mistakes people made while at other times, we discover role models of faith, obedience, and courage. We can also be encouraged by the poetry, songs, or diaries of the various biblical writers. Then there are times when we are warned of sin or spiritual apathy confronted by the prophets. In the New Testament, we can be inspired by the teachings of Jesus and the events surrounding the Early Church and the apostles. Even though the Bible contains different kinds of writings, it is all inspired by the same Holy Spirit; and because it is inspired, the Bible is a reliable standard for how we can live our own lives.

Let me take a few minutes to give you reasons why you should read the Bible every day.

The Bible gives us practical instruction. Have you ever tried to put something together without an instruction manual? It is frustrating. God's Word gives us practical coaching on every essential area of our lives. It teaches us about priorities, worry, marriage, relationships, sex, money, children, food, health, work, planning, science, parenting, nature, and nearly every other subject you can think of.

The Bible helps us solve our problems. God's Word is like a moral and spiritual compass when we are lost or headed in the wrong direction. The same Holy Spirit that inspired the biblical writers can speak to your heart about how you should apply it to your own life and situations. The Word of God convicts us, speaks powerfully to our hearts, and shows us how to get back on the right track. That is what Hebrews 4:12 means when it says, "For the word of God is alive and active. Sharper than any double-edged sword, it penetrates even to dividing soul and spirit, joints and marrow; it judges the thoughts and attitudes of the heart."

The Bible is like a personal spiritual coach who helps you grow. That is why the Apostle Paul encouraged young leaders to continue reading God's Word: "The Holy Scriptures, which are able to make you wise for salvation through faith in Christ Jesus. All Scripture is God-breathed and is useful for teaching, rebuking, correcting and training in righteousness" (2 Timothy 3:15-16).

The Bible is packed with spiritual power. Unlike other books, the Bible is pregnant with supernatural authority and a well of spiritual life. "For the word of God is alive and powerful. It is sharper than the sharpest two-edged sword, cutting between soul and spirit, between joint and marrow" (Hebrews 4:12 NLT).

The Bible feeds your spirit and nurtures your soul. Jesus compared the Scriptures to spiritual food when He said: "People do not live by bread alone, but by every word that comes from the mouth of God" (Matthew 4:4 NLT).

The Bible is to your spiritual health what food is to your body, what oxygen is to your lungs, and what gas is to your car. Listening to sermons and teachings on God's Word is not enough to keep you strong. You need to learn to read it yourself and feed your own spirit. That is why daily Bible reading is so important. The 15 to 20 minutes it takes to read those three chapters every day may be the most important thing you do.

We will talk more about this tomorrow, and I will give you a brief overview of the Bible. In the meantime, keep focused on the journey.

Day 6 Reflection Questions

- How will thinking of the Bible as "alive" and "active" change the way you read it?

- What challenges or obstacles might keep you from reading the Bible on a daily basis? How can you be proactive to overcome those?

- Jesus said that after His death and resurrection, He would send the Holy Spirit to guide each of His followers in truth (John 16:13); and He has carried out that promise! How does it feel to know that God's Holy Spirit is guiding you even as you read His Word?

- Have you already joined a Bible study at your local church? If not, give them a call today and find out how you can do so!

Day 7: An Overview of the Bible

Today is Day 7 of your journey, and the daily Bible reading is John 19-21. Have you read it yet? If not, be sure to carve out the time to allow God's Word to feed your spirit. That is what priorities are all about—making time for the important things in life.

Yesterday we talked about why the Bible is so important. Today I want to give you a quick overview of the Bible. The Christian Bible is divided into two parts. The first is called the Old Testament which contains 39 books, and the second portion is called the New Testament which contains 27 books.

Let's start by talking about the Old Testament. The 39 books of the Old Testament were written over a period of approximately a thousand years. Its books can be broken down into four categories:

- **The Pentateuch:** The word sounds complicated, but it means "five volumes"; and these five books are mostly narrative stories and details about the laws and precepts God gave to the nation of Israel. If you like novels, then you will love these stories.
- **The historical books:** These books contain the narrative stories that follow Israel's ups and downs as a nation.

- **Poetry and wisdom literature:** These are the poetic books such as Job, Psalms, and Proverbs as well as others.
- **The Prophets:** These books record the life and ministry of the prophets who lived during Israel's history as well as how God spoke through them to address the nation's spiritual pulse.

The New Testament. The 27 books of the New Testament were written over a period of approximately 70 years. Its books can be broken down into five categories:

- **The Gospels:** The gospels of Matthew, Mark, Luke, and John are four different accounts of the life and ministry of Jesus from four different perspectives.
- **Acts:** The Book of Acts is a record of the church after the resurrection of Christ.
- **The Pauline Letters:** These are letters the Apostle Paul wrote to Christian churches that were scattered around the Mediterranean and the Middle East. They address practical issues of everyday life and the church.
- **General Letters:** These are letters written by other apostles apart from Paul.
- **Apocalyptic literature:** This consists of the Book of Revelation which portrays God's ultimate victory over death, sin, and the devil.

You have probably heard people reference books, chapters, and verses of the Bible. I remember how confused I was the first time I heard people use abbreviated references to the Bible. What is Heb. 4:14 (Heb-dot-4-colon-14) anyway? A freeway? A Facebook password? Maybe a chemical element on the periodic table?

Let me explain. Heb. is an abbreviation for Hebrews, a book in the New Testament. You will find its location by looking it up in the Table of Contents in the front of your Bible which will show the page number on which the Book of Hebrews begins. The numbers separated by a colon refer to the chapter and verse. The chapter is before the colon and the verse is after it. Each chapter has many verses, usually only a sentence or two long, so Hebrews 4:14 would refer to the Book of Hebrews, Chapter 4, verse 14.

You might also be wondering why there are different English translations of the Bible. The original manuscripts of the Bible were written in three different languages. The Old Testament was originally written in Hebrew and a very small portion in Aramaic. The New Testament was originally written in Greek. Over the years, biblical scholars have mastered these languages so they could translate the Bible into modern English. That is why there are so many different versions of the English translations.

These translations usually come in two forms: a translation and a paraphrase. A translation strives for an accurate rendering of the original language without going beyond what was said in the original. On the other hand, a paraphrase only seeks to communicate general concepts or meanings of the original language.

If you do not already have a Bible, I would recommend you get the English Standard Version (ESV) translation. It is a modern translation that represents a huge pool of very gifted international scholars. If you want a more conversational version, try the New Living Translation (NLT).

As you read the Bible, you may have lots of questions. Well, I have good news for you. Study Bibles are special Bibles that have lots of helpful resources in the margins. These added resources usually include explanations about hard-to-understand verses, lists of similar verses, topical lists, Bible dictionaries, maps, and lots of other helpful resources. Although these notes are not part of Scripture, they can be helpful in satisfying your curiosity as you read. One of the best study Bibles available today is the NIV Study Bible. I use mine every day. If you do not have a Bible, I would recommend talking to your pastor who, I am certain, will be happy to get you one.

Tomorrow I am going to teach you how to read the Bible and get something out of it every time. If you will do the simple steps outlined, I can promise you will double your effectiveness in interacting with God's Word. We will talk more about that tomorrow.

Day 7 Reflection Questions

- Do you have your own, physical copy of the Bible in a translation you can easily understand? If not, ask the people at your local church how you can get one!

- Are you familiar with the different books in the Bible? Spend a few minutes using the Table of Contents to learn their names, abbreviations, and relative locations.

- What did you learn about the Bible today? Did anything surprise you about how it was written, formed, or passed down?

- Think about yesterday's conversation. How can the Bible tell a unified story if it was written by many human

Day 8: How to Read the Bible

Welcome to Day 8. Today's Bible reading is Acts 1-3.

Did you notice in today's Bible reading that Acts 2:42 tells us that the first Christians were devoted to the apostles' teaching? Do you know what those teachings were? We have the apostles' teaching bound in one book called the Bible! It was a priority for them, and it needs to be a priority for us as well.

Over the past few days, we have been talking about the importance of God's Word. Today I want to give you some of the most practical advice you will ever get about how to get the most out of your Bible reading. Before we do that, however, I want to make you a promise that I can keep. If you apply these five simple principles, you will double the effectiveness of your Bible reading. It is that simple, and it works.

The first thing you need to do is to view your daily Bible reading as an appointment with an important person. Don't think that Bible reading will happen on its own or that extra time will just drop out of the sky. You need to make it a priority. The best way to do that is to pick a regular time each and every day and make that your daily appointment with God. Make sure it is at a time when you are more likely to be alert, free from interruptions, and able to spend time thinking about what you read. View that time as a nonnegotiable daily appointment on your calendar. Nothing crowds it out or takes priority over it.

The second thing you need to do is adopt a reading plan. The Bible is a big book which contains 1,189 chapters. If you read:

- 1 verse a day, it would take you 85 years to read through the Bible.
- 1 chapter a day, it would take you 3 years and 2 months to read through the Bible.
- 2 chapters a day, it would take you 1 year and 8 months to read through the Bible.
- 3.5 chapters a day, it would take you one year to read through the Bible.
- 10 chapters a day, you could read through the Bible 3 times in one year.

You really need to read the entire Bible at least once every 16 months in order to to grasp its themes, appreciate it as a whole, and remember its important truths. The 1,189 chapters might seem like a lot, but chapters in the Bible are not as long as chapters you would normally find in a novel. As a matter of fact, the average person can read three chapters of the Bible in about 15-18 minutes. I call it the "Power of 3 Bible Reading Plan." The name means 3 chapters of the Bible each day. Right now, you are on a plan that focuses on the teachings of Jesus and the basic principles of the Christian faith; but after you finish this 30-day journey, you should consider continuing your reading though the entire Bible.

The third thing you need to do is read. However, don't read those three chapters quickly just to say you got it done. Read them slowly to yourself. As you read, underline verses or thoughts that speak to you in a special way, stir your interest, or apply to your own situation. On the other hand, don't get so bogged down that you cannot finish that day's three chapters. When you are done, you should have several verses underlined. Now you are ready to really experience spiritual growth!

The fourth thing you need to do is isolate one verse. This is very important. Never, and I mean never, leave the reading of God's Word without isolating one verse to focus on. This is easier than you may think. Just look back over the three chapters you have read and the verses you have underlined and then force yourself to pick one of those verses to claim as your "verse for the day." Jot the book, chapter, and verse number on a piece of paper and put it in your pocket. Use dead time or moments of inactivity throughout the day to think about that verse and how God might want you to apply this truth to your life. This is where most Christians miss it. They race through their Bible reading without ever taking something away. Never leave your Bible reading without claiming a verse!

The fifth and final thing you need to do is apply God's Word. This is what the Bible means when it says: "Do not merely listen to the word, and so deceive yourselves. Do what it says. Anyone who listens to the word but does not do what it says is like a man who looks at his face in a mirror and, after looking at himself, goes away and immediately forgets what he looks like" (James 1:22-24).

Following are some great questions to ask yourself about your verse for the day:
- Lord, what are you saying to me?
- Is there a promise for me to claim?

- Is there an example I should follow?
- Is there some sin or weakness I need to avoid?
- Is there a command for me to obey?
- Is there any new thought about God, Jesus, or the Holy Spirit that I need to adopt?

The key to daily Bible reading is having "reasonable habits." In other words, habits that are not exaggerated but realistic and doable on a daily basis. That is why the Power of 3 approach of reading three chapters a day has changed so many people's lives. It is simple, sustainable, and it works!

If you do these five simple things, your life will never be the same! If you get behind in your reading plan, don't get bogged down by guilt. Just pick right back up on the current date. If there are days that nothing magical seems to be happening, keep at it and don't give up. Give God your best time, your best thoughts, and your best effort; and He will bless you for it.

Tomorrow we are going to talk about prayer and how it affects your journey.

Day 8 Reflection Questions

- Take a look at your daily routine or schedule. Where can you make space for a daily appointment with God?
- Do you normally develop habits easily or with difficulty? Based on those past experiences, what can you do to establish this new daily discipline successfully?

- How can you maintain focus while you read the Bible? Perhaps by using a highlighter, jotting down notes, or something else?

- Why do think it is important to take a verse with you so that you can think about it throughout the day?

- After selecting one verse from today's reading (Acts 1-3), ask yourself, "Why did I hone in on this particular verse?"

Day 9: A Simple Way to Pray

Well, how are you doing? Are you being faithful to your daily appointment with God? Today is Day 9, and our Bible reading is Acts 4-6.

Did you notice in Acts 4:23 that the early church turned to God in prayer when they faced obstacles? The story is proof that prayer works, but sometimes it is easier to talk about prayer than it is to actually pray.

Many people feel uneasy about prayer for several reasons. For some, prayer is as awkward as writing with the wrong hand. Others feel unworthy or inadequate. Some feel guilty for not wanting to pray. If you feel uncomfortable praying, it may be that you are thinking about prayer in the wrong way. You don't have a problem talking to your closest friends, do you? Of course not. Conversation is easy and natural. That is how prayer should be—casual, comfortable, and conversational. The good news is that God wants us to pray and is eager to answer our prayers.

That is why I want to give you an easy way to remember how to pray. It is patterned after the way Jesus taught us to pray the Lord's Prayer in Matthew 6:9-13. The pattern is easy to remember because it follows the acronym: ACTS.

A stands for adoration. Adoration is worship or, as I like to call it, "worthship." That is what worship is—telling God how much He is worth to you. Don't start your prayer by talking about what you want; start your prayer by worshiping God for who He is, for what He has done in your life, and for what He is doing.

C stands for confession. Confession is admitting our sins and asking God's forgiveness. You might be wondering why that is necessary if Jesus died for our sins already. The answer is simple. Confession cuts sin off at the pass and robs it of its power in our lives. It humbly takes responsibility for our bad choices and recognizes that we need God's help, strength, and forgiveness to overcome them.

T stands for thanksgiving. Thanksgiving is taking the time to notice and thank God for all the things He has done for you. Some people treat God like an ATM machine. The only time they visit is when they want something, but thanksgiving is what keeps our spiritual lives from becoming self-absorbed and self-centered.

S stands for supplication. The word supplication means to "ask for something." James states: "You do not have because you do not ask God" (James 4:2). Isn't it liberating for us to know that God wants to bless us and meet our needs? If you have needs, then be specific and ask God to meet them.

If your prayers do not seem to be making a difference, don't give up. God is a lot smarter than we are. There may be many reasons why your answers to prayer seem delayed.

- It may be because the timing is not right. God might be waiting for you and the situation to be ready for an answer.

- Sometimes God wants the situation to mature to a point where His glory is maximized.
- At other times, a delay will increase your sense of urgency and elevate the intensity of your faith. This hyper-charged faith can lead you into deeper levels of maturity.
- There are other times that God uses a delay in answering your prayers to give you time to get your heart and priorities right.
- However, one of the most common reasons for unanswered prayer is that our desperation brings us closer to God.

I would encourage you to set aside quiet time each day and use this simple plan for prayer. It could be during your drive to or from work, alone in your office during lunch, while you exercise, or even when you take a quiet walk around your neighborhood. Where you pray is not as important as whether you pray, but the best way to learn to pray is to pray. Use the ACTS outline and start your daily prayer time.

Tomorrow I want to talk to you about sin, what it is, and how we can master it. Until then, continue the journey and don't forget to read God's Word.

Day 9 Reflection Questions

- Does prayer seem awkward or difficult? Why?
- God wants to hear from us and respond to us! What does that tell you about His character?
- How can you create space and time in your life to converse with God in prayer?

- In today's reading, you will find the believers praying together and God responding (Acts 4:23-31). What does this story teach you about prayer?

Day 10: Sin — Malware of the Soul

Welcome to Day 10 of your new journey! Today our Bible reading is Acts 7-9. These chapters introduce us to a religious man named Saul who had to learn that trying to be a good person could not resolve the spiritual problem of sin. After his conversion, Saul's name was changed to Paul; and he ends up being one of the most eloquent spokesmen for salvation by grace and not by works in the entire Bible. Like him, we all must learn that sin is a bigger problem than we realize.

Before you made a commitment to Christ, you probably were not as aware of sin as you are now; but now that you have begun your journey with Christ, the Holy Spirit has made you more sensitive to sin.

The most common misconception about sin is that it is a specific action or deed, such as lying, cheating, committing adultery, or even doing something dark like murder; but sin comes from something much deeper. Like a cough or a runny nose, the acts of sin are only symptoms of an internal spiritual infection.

The Bible tells us that sin comes from something embedded in our fallen nature. Sin is a virus that attacked mankind's soul way back in the Garden of Eden. It now manifests itself as an attitude deep within us that places our own desires before God's. It is that part of us that wants us to follow our own values and live independently of God's desired plan and purpose for our lives. Like malware on your computer's hard drive, sin wants to take control of your life and destroy everything it comes in contact with.

SIN (singular form) is the part of us that wants to disobey God. SINS (plural form) are the actions that SIN produces. The world tries to deal with SINS on a cosmetic level, but God is the only one who deals with SIN as a cause rather than a consequence. Let me explain.

God created us in His image with the ability to make choices. God loved us so much that He gave His creation the ability to choose, even if that choice was to reject Him. God warned Adam about the consequences of choosing sin, but he and Eve chose to rebel and accept those consequences. Ever since, the virus of sin was set loose in the human spirit. That is why our inclination towards selfishness, sin, and spiritual rebellion can be traced all the way back to the Garden of Eden in Genesis.

The nature of sin has now been passed down to each one of us. That is why, on our own, even the best of us is not completely sinless. No matter how minor or major our SINS may be, SIN has still infected our spiritual hard drive. That what the Bible means when it says that "when Adam sinned, sin entered the world. Adam's sin brought death, so death spread to everyone, for everyone sinned" (Romans 5:12 NLT).

The Bible also affirms this in many other verses: "For everyone has sinned; we all fall short of God's glorious standard" (Romans 3:23 NLT); "Your iniquities have separated you from your God; your sins have hidden his face from you, so that he will not hear" (Isaiah 59:2); "There is no one righteous, not even one; there is no one who understands; no one who seeks God. All have turned away, they have together become worthless; there is no one who does good, not even one" (Romans 3:10-12).

That is why God is the only one capable of saving us because He is the only one immune to the virus of sin; but if God is the only one who can save us, we need to remember who instigated this problem of sin in the first place. That is where things get interesting.

We have a spiritual adversary, an opponent. The Bible calls him Satan or the devil. As a fallen angel, he is not satisfied just with Adam and Eve's failure. He is dangerous and wants you to share in his spiritual misery. If you study the teachings of Jesus, you will find that He said more about Satan than anyone else in the entire Bible; but sin is not undefeatable! Remember, God created us in His image with the power to choose. Choice is the one quality we share with God that can always lead us back to Him.

Before Jesus began His earthly ministry, He spent a significant amount of time in the mountains praying. It was there that Satan tempted Him three times. This is recorded in Luke 4:1-13 where Satan tempted Jesus to put His physical needs, pride, and purpose before God's desires. Satan and his demons do not have the power to steal us from God, but they do try to convince us to exercise the power of choice to defy and rebel against God. Satan knows that our God-given power of choice is the only way to defeat us.

That is why God did not leave you powerless against Satan. The Holy Spirit can help you. The key is in refusing to satisfy your sin nature and instead feed your godly desires.

Tomorrow we will talk more about how to overcome temptation; but for now, it is important that you understand the difference between SIN and SINS and how those two things relate to your power of choice. We will talk more tomorrow.

Day 10 Reflection Questions

- Have you noticed a greater sensitivity to sin in your own life? What has that experience been like?
- How would you explain the difference between "sin" and "sins" to someone if they asked you about it?
- Why is it important to understand that all have sinned, that no one is righteous?
- What has God done to save us from sin and help us live righteously?
- How might the story of Saul's conversion (Acts 9) encourage someone who thinks they have sinned too much to be forgiven?

Day 11: Overcoming Temptation

Welcome to Day 11 of your new journey. Our Bible reading for today is Acts 10-12.

Have you noticed there are two sides to you—one side wants to please God and the other side wants to please yourself? One side that wants to read the Bible and the other side that does not? Even the Apostle Paul battled with this and made a very transparent confession: "For I have the desire to do what is good, but I cannot carry it out. For I do not do the good I want to do, but the evil I do not want to do—this I keep on doing" (Romans 7:18-19).

It reminds me of the story of Dr. Jekyll and Mr. Hyde. Dr. Jekyll develops a drug that unchains the evil side of his nature. His good side is called "Jekyll" and his evil side is called "Hyde." The book describes his struggle with these dual natures—usually very good but sometimes shockingly evil. In a sense, that is what you and I have inside us. The Bible calls the one "spirit" and the other "flesh."

Before you became a Christ-follower, your old nature (the flesh) is what directed your thoughts, motives, and priorities; but when you became a Christ-follower, Christ broke the power of your flesh and breathed life into a new spirit within you. That is what the Bible means when it says: "Anyone who belongs to Christ has become a new person. The old life is gone; a new life has begun!" (2 Corinthians 5:17 NLT).

Your old, dead spirit has been made alive in Christ and now desires spiritual things. Since you have become a follower of Christ, you have an increased sensitivity to spiritual things like God, sin, and the Bible. You have a new desire to please God and do not want to disappoint Him.

On the other hand, the flesh is the part of us that is ruled by our sinful nature. It craves everything that God is not. Notice that the Bible says both of these things have desires: "Walk by the Spirit, and you will not gratify the desires of the flesh. For the flesh desires what is contrary to the Spirit, and the Spirit what is contrary to the flesh. They are in conflict with each other, so that you are not to do whatever you want" (Galatians 5:16-17).

Paul compares each of these competing desires to a field and seeds. He urges us to remember that whatever we feed grows: "Do not be deceived: God cannot be mocked. A man reaps what he sows. Whoever sows to please their flesh, from the flesh will reap destruction; whoever sows to please the Spirit, from the Spirit will reap eternal life" (Galatians 6:7-8).

I like to compare the image to two baby birds in a nest. One is spirit and the other is our sinful nature. Both are present, active, and very much alive. Both are chirping loudly to get our attention and are asking us to satisfy their cravings and desires. Both oppose and contradict each other, and both want leadership of our life.

Temptation happens when a desire of the sinful nature is presented with an opportunity to satisfy its appetite. Let me give you six helpful tips in dealing with temptation or the loud chirping of the flesh, as I like to call it.

Sin is not an address; it is a neighborhood. We never wake up and find ourselves at the doorstep of sin without first wandering into the neighborhood. That is why it is important that you do not allow yourself to get into a situation where you are likely to sin. A person who is allergic to peanuts does not hang out in a peanut factory or in a restaurant with peanut shells all over the floor. That's what the Bible means when it says: "Resist the devil, and he will flee from you" (James 4:7).

Whatever you feed, grows. If your temptation seems stronger than your godly desires, it is because you are feeding it. The key is to starve the sinful nature and feed the spirit. How can you keep your spirit fed, nourished, and strong? Read your Bible every day, hang out with Christians who bring out the best in you, and respond quickly when the Holy Spirit convicts you of sin. When that godly nature asks you to feed it by doing things that build your spirit, then do it! Why? Because whatever you feed, grows.

Become familiar with Scripture. When Jesus was tempted by Satan, do you know what His number one weapon of defense was? The Bible! Every time the devil tempted Him, Jesus responded by quoting Scriptures that He had previously read and studied. Luke 4:1-13 shows us that Jesus's familiarity with Scripture made Him successful over temptation. It is an encouraging passage to read.

Pray and ask God for strength. When Jesus prayed in the Garden of Gethsemane, He struggled with the inevitable and unavoidable reality of His crucifixion; but the Bible tells us that after He prayed, He was given renewed strength and courage to face the future. Prayer can do the same thing for us. That is why the Bible reminds us that "greater is He who is in you than he who is in the world" (1 John 4:4 NASB).

Make yourself accountable to others. The Bible tells us to surround ourselves with those who bring out the best in us instead of the worst. Find Christian friends who are more spiritually mature than you and invest in a transparent and rewarding relationship. They can pray with and for you during these difficult times. The Bible affirms this when it says that "bad company corrupts good character" (1 Corinthians 15:33).

Seek God's forgiveness when you fail. Listen! There are going to be times when you will sin and will need God's forgiveness and strength. We are going to talk more about this tomorrow, but it is important to state now that repentance is important for spiritual growth.

So what if we keep on sinning after becoming a Christian? Tomorrow we are going to talk about what to do when we fail. Until then, remember to feed the spirit and starve the flesh. Overcoming temptation is all about feeding the right thing.

Day 11 Reflection Questions

- In what sense are you a "new creation" since giving your life to Jesus?
- Why do we, as Christians, still find ourselves fighting off old sins and bad habits?
- How can you "feed" your spirit and "starve" your flesh?

- Who are some Christian friends in your life who could help you become stronger and fight off sin?
- Think through what you have read in Acts. How did the first Christians work together to glorify God in everything they did rather than satisfying selfish desires or old sinful habits?

Day 12: What If I Sin?

Today is Day 12 of your new journey, and our Bible reading is Acts 13-15. I bet you can feel your faith and understanding of God growing each day!

Yesterday we talked about how to overcome temptation, but today I want to talk to you about what to do when you sin. It's good if you feel convicted after you sin, but don't let the devil make you feel unworthy of God's forgiveness. I think that is what the Apostle John was talking about when he wrote: "My dear children, I write this to you so that you will not sin. But if anybody does sin, we have an advocate with the Father—Jesus Christ, the Righteous One. He is the atoning sacrifice for our sins, and not only for ours but also for the sins of the whole world" (1 John 2:1-2).

Did you catch what John said? He said Christ's sacrifice and forgiveness is not a disposable cup that can only be used once. It is a well of forgiveness, grace, and strength for our entire lives. The Bible also makes this promise to us: "If we confess our sins, he is faithful and just and will forgive us our sins and purify us from all unrighteousness" (1 John 1:9).

So what do these verses teach us about what to do when we fail? A lot!

The first thing we need to do is repent. Repentance is being sorry that we let God down and not just sorry that we got "caught." That is what the Bible means when it says that "godly sorrow brings repentance" (2 Corinthians 7:10). It is mentally and emotionally recognizing that we have grieved God's Spirit. When we humbly confess our sin to God and own our actions, we drain sin of its power.

The second thing we need to do is confess. Confession is recognizing our need for grace. God does not require confession because He is insecure and likes to see us grovel. He requires confession because it is more valuable to us than to Him. Confession is the result of someone's being mature enough to take responsibly for their actions instead of looking for someone or something else to blame. Excuses are often pride disguised as humility.

The third thing we need to do is seek God's forgiveness. Forgiveness is free, but it must be sought and accepted. One of the oldest tricks the devil uses to distract us is to make us think we are unworthy of forgiveness and grace. We may still believe that God is forgiving, gracious, and merciful to others—but not to us. That is what the devil wants you to believe—that God's forgiveness is for everyone else BUT you! That is why the Bible makes us this promise: "If we confess our sins, he is faithful and just and will forgive us our sins and purify us from all unrighteousness" (1 John 1:9).

The fourth thing we need to do is recognize that temptation is not sin. Jesus was severely tempted, but the Bible tells us He was without sin. I love what Martin Luther, the German theologian and religious reformer who was the catalyst of the sixteenth-century Protestant Reformation, said about this: "You can't help it if a bird flies over your head, but you can stop it from building a nest in your hair." In the same way, we need to recognize temptation before it grows into sin.

Sin can be so disappointing to us, but the fact that you are disappointed after you sin is a good thing. It is when you sin and are not disappointed, sad, or grieved that you really need to be concerned. That is a scary place to be! The encouraging thing is that the more you mature in your faith, the stronger you will become; and the stronger you become, the easier it will be to resist temptation. Remember that whatever you feed, grows so feed the spirit and continue the journey.

Tomorrow I want to talk to you about why church is so important to your spiritual growth. We will talk more then.

Day 12 Reflection Questions

- What is the difference between feeling convicted of sin and feeling unworthy of forgiveness?
- How would you describe the experience of conviction?
- When the Holy Spirit has pointed out sin in your life, what did it feel like?
- Why does God ask us to admit our sins to Him?
- What is the relationship between temptation and sin? Are they the same thing?
- Today you came across Acts 13:38 which reads, "through Jesus the forgiveness of sins is proclaimed to you." What makes forgiveness in Jesus such good news?

Day 13: Is Church Important?

Welcome to Day 13. Our Bible reading is Acts 16-18. In these three chapters, we see the early believers growing in their faith and becoming connected to smaller communities of faith. It is in these church gatherings that their faith was strengthened and their knowledge of God's Word matured. It begs the question that if faith is about our relationship with God, then why is attending church and being part of a local community of faith important? That question deserves a thoughtful response.

Science tells us that fusion is the process by which individual parts become strengthened by their connection to the whole. The same thing happens to us spiritually when we join a community of faith and attend church. As a matter of fact, some Christians in biblical times began to neglect church attendance. Hebrews 10:25 confronts this tendency head-on when it commands us "not to give up meeting together, as some are in the habit of doing, but to encourage one another—and all the more as you see the Day approaching."

This short verse gives us four simple reasons why belonging to a local community of faith and church attendance is important for spiritual growth.

The first reason is that you should want to obey God. The only motivation we should need for being faithful in church attendance is that God commanded it. This verse makes it perfectly clear that God wants us to make church attendance a priority. That is why King David told God that "a single day in your courts is better than a thousand anywhere else! I would rather be a gatekeeper in the house of my God than live the good life" (Psalm 84:10 NLT). King David was a busy man with an entire kingdom to run; but of all the places he could be, he wanted to be worshiping with God's people.

The second reason is that attending church and worshiping with other believers is rewarding. Did you notice that Hebrews 10:25 is encouraging habits that are the opposite of neglect? Why? Because church is one of those habits that makes us stronger, not weaker; and there are so many reasons why:

- It is where God's presence can be experienced with and among His people.
- It is where you have access to the people who are uniquely gifted and trained to help you grow spiritually.
- It is where you find belonging, support, and encouragement on your spiritual journey.
- It is where you receive practical teaching on how to follow God.
- It is where you are part of something bigger than yourself.
- It is where you can use your spiritual gifts, talents, and abilities to help others.

In light of all these benefits, few things will nurture your spiritual growth like regular church attendance.

The third reason is that developing the habit of participating in church is also energizing! There is a supernatural synergy that happens when people worship together. When Hebrews 10:25 uses the phrase "encouraging one another," it is telling us that something powerful happens in all of us when we worship together. That means you are not the only one benefiting when you attend church. Your presence, worship, and participation become a powerful force that builds up the lives of other Christians as well.

Did you know that the Bible tells us that the presence of God is most easily encountered in times of public praise and prayer? When God's people gather in worship, prayer, and teaching, God is present in their midst in a special way. That is what Jesus was talking about when He said: "For where two or three gather in my name, there am I with them" (Matthew 18:20).

The Bible has revealed three reasons why your faithfulness to church is important, but there is a fourth reason that gets a little sobering. People have said to me, "Come on. We live in a different culture. People are busy, and the chaos of our times warrants downsizing our commitment to church." The Bible tells us the exact opposite. It says that we will need the church more and more the closer we get to the end-times and the Second Coming of Christ. That is what Hebrews 10:25 means when it says that we are "not to give up meeting together . . . and all the more as we see the Day approaching." In other words, gathering together for church will become more needful and more valuable the closer we get to the return of Christ! What does this mean? It means that the closer we get to the end-times, the harder it will become to be a Christian. It means the end-times will demand a strength that will only come through being an active part of a community of faith. It means we need each other more, not less. It means time is limited, and we must be strengthened by gathering together in worship, teaching, and prayer.

The Bible is literally pleading with people not to make the mistake of neglecting church. Why? Because God knows that without it, we cannot survive. We will talk more about this tomorrow.

Day 13 Reflection Questions

- Why is church attendance so crucial when it comes to spiritual growth?
- How will your presence in the local church bless other believers? Have you ever looked at church attendance that way before?
- What benefits do you see in connecting with other followers of Jesus?
- How would following Jesus become more challenging without the support of a local church?
- Take another look at Acts 16-18. Where do you see churches coming together as Paul and Silas preach from city to city? Who is strengthened by a local community of believers?

Day 14: Getting the Most Out of Church

How are you doing on your daily Bible reading? This is Day 14 of your journey, and today's Bible reading is Acts 19-21. One of the things I love about these three chapters is the story concerning the young man who fell asleep during a very long church service. Apparently, the service went so long that he fell asleep and tumbled from a ledge and died. Paul prayed for him, and God brought the boy back to life. Talk about getting a lot out of a church service!

The word "more" is a favorite word for advertisers. Why? Because they know we all want it! We want more mileage per gallon, more bang for our buck, more house for our money, and more memory in our electronic devices. We want the "most" out of everything else in life so why not church? I wish someone had talked to me about this after I became a follower of Christ. This is why I want to get practical and give you some tips on how to get the most out of a church service.

The first thing we need to do is make spiritual growth a priority. We see this in the lives of the very first Christians: "They devoted themselves to the apostles' teaching and to the fellowship, to the breaking of bread and to prayer" (Acts 2:42). This Scripture is talking about being devoted, committed, and consistent in your spiritual growth. Why? Because without commitment, your faith will never move past good intentions or survive tough times. This is why I want you to decide right now—at the beginning of your journey—that no matter how busy you get, you are going to attend three out of four Sunday morning church services a month. Goal #1: Attend three out of four church services a month.

The second thing you need to do is have high expectations. Come to church expecting God to do something new and exciting in your life! James speaks about the importance of expecting great things from God: "But when you ask him, be sure that your faith is in God alone. Do not waver, for a person with divided loyalty is as unsettled as a wave of the sea that is blown and tossed by the wind. Such people should not expect to receive anything from the Lord" (James 1:6-7 NLT). That means you should view church as an opportunity, not an obligation. Goal #2: Raise the level of your expectations.

The third thing you need to do is eliminate distractions. There is a great proverb that says it is "the little foxes that ruin the vineyards" (Song of Songs 2:15). I love that analogy! There are a lot of "little foxes" that can rob us of spiritual opportunities. The "little foxes" make us disengaged, disconnected, and distracted while attending church on Sunday morning—things like:

- Coming late, going in and out of the service, and leaving early.
- Being distracted by your cell phone, text messages, emails, or activity on social media.
- Sitting by yourself in an isolated section of the auditorium.
- Concentrating on other things that need to be done that week, problems, or even the football game after church.

So be on the lookout for the little foxes! They are inconspicuous, fast, and barely noticeable; but they rob you of the wonderful things that are waiting for you at church. Goal #3: Don't get distracted!

The fourth thing you need to do is participate. Arrive early to talk to others, introduce yourself, and learn people's names. During worship, don't just sit back and be a passive spectator. Engage and participate. We often think of the pastors and the worship band as the performers and ourselves as the audience. In reality, worship is for God, not us. We are the performers, and God is the audience. During times of prayer, don't be afraid to let others pray with and for you about your needs. If you see others receiving prayer, pray for them in your seat. Remember, we are all in this together! Goal # 4: Be a participant, not a spectator.

The fifth thing you need to do is engage in the teaching of God's Word. The Bible teaches us that God has called, gifted, and anointed pastors for the specific purpose of building up our faith. By the time you hear a 30-minute teaching, over 20 hours of prayer, research, study, writing, and creative efforts have gone into its preparation. Teaching can grow your faith for "faith comes from hearing the message, and the message is heard through the word about Christ" (Romans 10:17). So take it all in by listening intently, taking notes, and thinking of ways you can act upon what you are hearing and learning. Goal #5: Apply God's Word to your life.

Church services are one of the greatest spiritual opportunities you will have all week. At your church, every service is planned with specific opportunities to respond and embrace truth. Be ready, willing, and eager to take advantage of them.

Tomorrow I want to talk to you about the one thing God does not want you to be silent about. More then.

Day 14 Reflection Questions

- How can you get the most out of church gatherings and worship services?
- Do you enter your church service or small group meeting with high expectations? Why or why not?
- What things might be keeping you from committing to gather and getting involved with other believers?
- Why do you think it is so important to see yourself as a participant in church rather than a spectator?
- In today's reading, you see God do some incredible things in unexpected ways—like resurrecting a young man during a church service! How has God comforted or strengthened you in surprising ways through the local church?

Day 15: Why Should I Tell People?

Today is Day 15, and our daily Bible reading is Acts 22-24. In these three chapters, we find Paul telling everyone about what God has done in his life. Like Paul, you have experienced spiritual transformation.

You have been a child of God for 15 days, but what if no one had ever told you about Christ? What if they were worried that you would be offended? What if whoever introduced you to Christ let fear keep them from telling you the most important thing you could ever hear? Aren't you glad they shared the good news with you? But what about those who have yet to hear about this new life you have experienced? Believe it or not, there are hundreds of people in your life who are in the very same position you were before Christ. They have yet to become a Christ-follower, and you may be the only one to tell them. Okay, I know what you are thinking. "I don't want to offend anyone."

In today's culture, religious tolerance is usually measured by what you DO NOT say rather than what you DO say. What if I were to tell you that Jesus wants and expects you to tell others about your experience with Him? He does not want your faith to be the best-kept secret in your life. Many Christians make the mistake of ignoring Jesus's command to talk with others about their experience with God. Why? There are several reasons.

Some Christians mistakenly think that living out their faith silently is all that God requires. They hope the curiosity of others will one day lead them to ask the right questions. Many think it is the church's responsibility to tell others about Christ so they wait for others to walk through the doors of a church where a pastor or church program will present the message of salvation. Many Christians do not share their faith because they are afraid people will think less of them. Some believers buy into the lie that they have to be an expert in the Bible before they are qualified to share their faith with others.

Not one of these reasons excuses us from Christ's command to talk with others about our faith. Well then, why does Jesus require us to share our faith? Why can't we just live out our faith privately? Let me give you three reasons why.

The first reason is because Jesus told us to, and He told us to do it in a big way. As a matter of fact, Jesus said to "go and make disciples of all nations" (Matthew 28:19). It was the last thing He said before leaving the earth and returning to heaven. Peter tells us to "always be prepared to give an answer to everyone who asks you to give the reason for the hope that you have" (1 Peter 3:15). Jesus compared our faith to a bright light that should shine before men so that they may know God (Matthew 5:16).

The second reason is because people need to hear it. Today you are reading this book and celebrating your 15th day of faith, but what if no one had told you about Christ? What if they were worried about offending you or hoped that you would somehow decipher the secret code behind their actions? What if they let you pass into a Christless eternity without ever telling you the good news about God's love? You get the picture. There are people just like you were who are separated from God and do not know how to find their way to Him. You are God's living love letter to people in your life. Your relationship with them is God's bridge of hope.

The third reason is because word of mouth works. People can argue with your philosophy, theology, or opinion; but they cannot argue with your personal experience. People will listen to someone whose passion has been ignited by an authentic experience. Nobody wants to hear about climbing a mountain and standing at the peak from someone who has never been there! Passion is contagious. That is why the Bible records the Apostle Paul repeatedly telling the story about how he came to Christ. Your experience is just that—your experience, and no argument is as powerful as someone's personal experience. That is why the Christian faith grew for the first hundred years without printed material, dedicated buildings, technology, or slick advertising. Why? Because the most effective message is a personal message!

Doctors swear to a professional code of ethics called the "Hippocratic oath." This oath holds them accountable to use their knowledge to help others who are in need. Christians are bound by an oath to a much higher authority. As Christ-followers, we are bound to share the most liberating truth the world has ever known—the saving knowledge of Jesus Christ.

In a future chapter, we will talk about what and how to share our faith; but for now, I want you to decide not to be a secret follower of Christ. I want you to resist the excuses that keep others in spiritual darkness and be willing to share your story when God presents an opportunity.

Tomorrow we will talk about exactly what to share and, the day after that, how to share it. For now, stay in God's Word and look for opportunities to tell your story.

Day 15 Reflection Questions

- Who told you about Jesus? How did they explain the good news to you? Give thanks to God for that interaction!
- We were all introduced to Jesus by someone! What keeps us from making that introduction to friends and family members who have not yet heard about him?
- Society tends to regard faith as private and personal. Why did Jesus command us to share our faith with others?
- What do you find most intimidating or challenging when it comes to telling others about Jesus? Who might be able to help you overcome those concerns?
- While reading Acts, you have seen how boldly the followers of Jesus proclaimed their faith. How do you think they were able to do that?

Day 16: What's the Good News?

Welcome to Day 16 of your journey. Today's Bible reading is Acts 25-27. In these chapters, we again see Paul sharing the good news about salvation with friends, neighbors, kings, political rulers, and just about anyone who will listen.

Yesterday we talked about why Christ wants us to tell others our story of faith, but what exactly are we to share with others? Is a normal person without formal theological training qualified to talk with others about God's love? Absolutely!

The biggest mistake you can make in this area is to think that God wants you to share some complex theological argument filled with scriptural quotations, argumentative strategy, or confrontational debate. Nothing can be farther from the truth! The message of the gospel was never meant to be a scripted debate or argument. It was and is meant to be "good news." As a matter of fact, that is what the word "gospel" actually means when it is used 98 times in the New Testament. It is meant to be GOOD NEWS!

So what is this good news about Jesus? Let me make it really simple.

God created us with freedom of choice. He created us in His image with the power to choose between right and wrong, but we used that freedom to choose something other than God. Instead of trusting Him, Adam and Eve chose sin, rebellion, and independence from God. Even though they had the freedom to choose any tree in the entire Garden, they chose the one tree God told them to avoid—the tree that gave them knowledge of evil. By doing that, they surrendered their freedom, exposed themselves to evil, and became chained by sin.

God's love provides a way out of sin's bondage. Even though we chose to rebel against God and to let sin separate us from Him, God never stopped loving us. His love made Him willing to make the most extreme sacrifices to save us. That is what the Apostle Paul meant when he said: "God demonstrates his own love for us in this: While we were still sinners, Christ died for us. Since we have now been justified by his blood, how much more shall we be saved from God's wrath through him! For if, while we were God's enemies, we were reconciled to him through the death of his Son, how much more, having been reconciled, shall we be saved through his life!" (Romans 5:8-10).

Our choice is now the only thing holding us back from our eternal purpose. The death and resurrection of Christ now means that God has once again placed our eternal destiny back within the sphere of choice. Because we have been created in the image of God as spiritual beings, our souls will live for eternity no matter what choice we make. Whether our existence is eternity with God or eternity separated from God depends upon whether we accept God's solution to the sin problem. That is what the Bible means in John 3:16: "For God so loved the world that he gave his one and only Son, that whoever believes in him shall not perish but have eternal life."

That is the good news in a nutshell. We surrendered our spiritual freedom for bondage to sin, and God became the solution by placing our eternal destiny back within the sphere of choice. That is good news so don't make the good news complicated! Don't turn the good news into bad news, controversial news, or alienating news. Keep it simple and to the point.

Tomorrow we will talk more about how to share our faith without being overbearing or rude. Until then, continue the journey.

Day 16 Reflection Questions

- How is telling others about Jesus more like sharing good news than starting a debate?
- Why don't we need formal training in theology or philosophy to start sharing the good news with others?
- Do you think everyone can, at least, relate to the gospel on the basis of their own bad choices and the brokenness they see in the world around them? Why?
- Who in your life might be open to hearing the good news about Jesus Christ?
- What can you learn about sharing your faith from today's reading in Acts 25-27?

Day 17: How to Share Your Faith

It is Day 17, and our Bible reading is Acts 28-Romans 2. In today's reading, we see Paul's bold and eager desire to share his faith with others. He tells us: "I am not ashamed of the gospel, because it is the power of God that brings salvation to everyone who believes" (Romans 1:16). Over the past two days, we have been talking about why sharing our faith is so important and what is important to share. Today I want to talk to you about how.

Once you become a Christ-follower, one of the most natural things you can do is to tell other people what Christ has done for you. Believe it or not, word of mouth is the primary way that the Christian faith spread to the farthest corners of our planet. Normal people experienced the grace of God and told others. As a matter of fact, the Book of Acts does not record one single instance of a person coming to faith simply by reading a brochure or watching a debate. Why? Because God wants His message to be personal, real, and down-to-earth.

Sharing your faith might seem intimidating or even unappealing to you right now. If it does, it may be because you have an inaccurate view of what God expects of you in this area. Let me explain.

Sharing your faith is not forcing your beliefs on someone, preaching a sermon, or even being responsible for whether someone actually decides to follow Christ. It is as simple as telling them what God has done for you and how your life has been changed as a result of it. This is the method the Apostle Paul used over and over again in sharing his own faith with those around him and why he said: "I am not ashamed of the gospel, because it is the power of God that brings salvation to everyone who believes" (Romans 1:16).

How did Paul share his faith? He did four simple things. Let's look at each one of them.

The first thing he did was to use creative ways to get people's attention. Both Paul and Jesus used all kinds of things around them as a springboard to talk about spiritual truths. Jesus used things like water, wells, fish, trees, towers, and anything else that was readily available. Paul used statues, court hearings, tents, marriage, citizenship, and many other things. You can do the same. I once read a book by Mike Silva called *Do You Want Fries With That?* Mike's book gives over 100 creative ways to talk about spiritual things without creeping people out. Some of the ideas were:

- Comparing God's forgiveness to a gift card that is useless unless it is redeemed.
- Comparing sin to clogged arteries that hinder us no matter how good we look on the outside.
- Using a watch to talk about how time is running out before the Lord returns.
- Using an old and wrinkled $20 bill to compare it to us. No matter what we have been through, we are still valuable to God.
- Defragmenting your computer to compare how God can straighten out the clutter in our lives.

You get the picture. Use simple, everyday things instead of complex theological thoughts as a springboard for discussion.

The second thing Paul did was to tell the "before and after" version of his life with Christ. Paul never grew weary of telling his story in creative ways. He told people details about what his life was like before God made a difference. He talked about his meaningless ambition, his propensity toward violence, and his spiritual heritage. In the same way, you can tell others your own "before and after" story about Christ. Tell them what your thoughts, perspective, home life, career, or relationships were like before God was at the center of your life. Be sure not to brag or exaggerate. Just be real and honest.

The third thing Paul did was to tell others how God got his attention. Paul captivated people by telling them how God used "shock and awe" to get his attention. In the same way, you could also tell people how you became convinced that sin was holding you back and how you reconciled your relationship with God. All believers have a critical point or trigger that God used to get their attention. Telling yours makes your faith story relevant to others.

The fourth thing Paul did was to describe the changes God brought to his life. Paul always closed his faith-filled conversations by telling people what his new life in Christ was like. For me, it was being delivered from drugs and living with a new sense of purpose and a passion to help others. In the same way, you should share details about how God has made a difference in the many areas of your life. It does not matter how great or small, the important thing is to help others understand that God can help them change.

Why not try it this week? God has sent many people into your life. Your relationships are not by chance. Friends, family, coworkers, school associates, neighbors, and people you know through recreational involvements may not know the good news of God's love; but you can tell them. Don't be longwinded or overbearing. View yourself as a witness of something instead of a debater trying to convince them that you are right. Be real and conversational and even honest about not having all the answers.

It is that simple. Just tell others about your past, present, and future with Christ. You will be amazed how easy it is and how open people are.

Tomorrow we are going to talk about the Holy Spirit. We will talk more then.

Day 17 Reflection Questions

- What did you think God expected of you when it came to sharing your faith? Were your assumptions correct?
- How can you put your own creativity to use when telling others about Jesus?
- Why do people respond so well to "before-and-after" stories? What would your "before-and-after" sound like?
- Where have you seen the biggest changes in your life overcome since deciding to follow Jesus? Who might be encouraged by hearing about those changes?
- Romans 1:16 says, "I am not ashamed of the gospel, because it is the power of God that brings salvation to everyone who believes." Why should we not be embarrassed to speak about all that Jesus has done?

Day 18: The Holy Spirit

Welcome to Day 18 of your journey. Today's Power of 3 reading is Romans 3-5.

I love what Paul says in Romans 5:5: "Hope does not put us to shame, because God's love has been poured out into our hearts through the Holy Spirit, who has been given to us." Paul teaches us that God has given us the Holy Spirit who pours God's love into our hearts!

The Holy Spirit is probably the least understood Person of the Trinity. And what about that word "trinity"? What does it mean? The word "trinity" comes from the Latin word, trinitas, meaning a triad or the number 3. The Trinity is a Christian term used to describe the One True God consisting of three different yet equal beings: the Father, the Son, and the Holy Spirit.

Although the word "Trinity" is not used in the Bible, the concept is represented in both the Old and New Testaments. When describing the creation of man, God said: "Let us make mankind in our image, in our likeness" (Genesis 1:26). Did you catch the reference God made to Himself in the third person plural? When describing himself, God used words like us, our image, and our likeness. When God says "our," He is referring to the Father, the Son, and the Holy Spirit; but God the Father is not the only one who claimed to be deity. Jesus claimed to be deity saying: "Before

Abraham was born, I am!" (John 8:58). Jesus is the image of the invisible God and was there and a part of creating the universe: "For in him all things were created: things in heaven and on earth, visible and invisible, whether thrones or powers or rulers or authorities; all things have been created through him and for him" (Colossians 1:16).

What about the Holy Spirit who is also described as being part of God: "The Spirit searches all things, even the deep things of God" (1 Corinthians 2:10).

The Trinity does not teach a multiplicity of gods. It points to distinctive aspects of one God from different perspectives. Each person of the Trinity has a distinct role to play. The Bible describes the role of the Father as the initiator of life, provider, and protector. Christ fulfills the role of redeemer and mediator. The Holy Spirit seems to provide internal power and communication between God and His creation.

Christians have struggled for centuries to understand the mystery of the Trinity. How can the Father, Son, and Holy Spirit be one and still be three persons? The Bible teaches us they are all equally God but, in some way, acting with different roles and functions. It is never easy to explain the mysteries of God; but when the Bible speaks of them as three in one, it is helpful to use the analogy of water, steam, and ice. All three are made up of the same chemical base but are different in form. The same can be said about the Father, Son, and Holy Spirit.

Why is the Holy Spirit so important to understand? The word "spirit" comes from a word meaning "breath" or "wind." The Bible describes the Holy Spirit as the breath of

God, unseen but powerful. Even if we cannot fully understand the Holy Spirit, the Bible teaches us that He is active in our lives. When you became a Christ-follower, the Holy Spirit was already working and moving in your life. Jesus told us that the Holy Spirit is NOT a passive or silent partner of the Trinity. As a matter of fact, the Holy Spirit has a very important role in the growth of your faith so let's talk for a few minutes about what that role is and how you can cooperate with the Holy Spirit as He leads and guides you.

Listen to the Holy Spirit when He makes you aware of sin. Even before you became a Christian, the Holy Spirit was speaking to your heart, drawing you to Christ, and calling you to Himself. Jesus told His disciples about this: "When he comes, he will prove the world to be in the wrong about sin and righteousness and judgment" (John 16:8). In a sense, the Holy Spirit is God's ambassador to our consciences and convinces us that we need God, that God wants to redeem us, and that we can trust God with our lives. That is why it is important to keep your heart and conscience sensitive to the Holy Spirit. The more you obey the voice of God's Spirit, the more you are able to discern and recognize it; but the more you ignore the Spirit's voice, the harder it is to hear it.

Satisfy the godly appetites that the Holy Spirit puts in your heart. God does not leave us without direction in a world of confusing options. The Holy Spirit reveals opportunities that lead to God as well as ones that lead away from God. He does this by giving us "spiritual cravings" or "godly appetites." Your ability to resist temptation gets stronger when you satisfy the cravings of God's Spirit and deprive the desires of your sinful nature. This is what the Bible means when it says: "Walk by the Spirit, and you will not gratify the desires of the flesh. For the flesh desires what is contrary to the Spirit, and the Spirit what is contrary to the flesh. They are in conflict with each other, so that you are not to do whatever you want. But if you are led by the Spirit, you are not under the law" (Galatians 5:16-18).

Rely on the Holy Spirit to access God's supernatural power. A religious leader named Nicodemus was trying to figure out how to achieve spiritual things in a natural way. Jesus warned him that spiritual things can only be accomplished on a spiritual level through the work of the Holy Spirit and told him that the "flesh gives birth to flesh, but the Spirit gives birth to spirit" (John 3:6). Remember that God created you in His image as a spiritual being and that part of you has been reborn and made alive to God. The Holy Spirit is our tour guide in helping us navigate and access our new life in the Spirit.

Make your heart a place where the Holy Spirit is welcome. In the Old Testament, the Spirit of God resided outside of man and on things, places, and people where God revealed himself. After Christ's resurrection, the Holy Spirit dwells in the hearts of God's people. The Holy Spirit is God in us working in full cooperation with the Father and the Son. It is not important to determine exactly whether the Holy Spirit or Jesus is doing something. Just realize that each has his own particular role in our lives.

Allow the Holy Spirit to make you more like Christ. Not only does the Holy Spirit open our lives up to the supernatural work of God, but He also exposes our lives to the character of God. Because the Holy Spirit is God's Spirit, He can help us develop the character of our heavenly Father. The Apostle Paul compares our hearts to a field that the Holy Spirit wants to plant seeds in: "The fruit of the Spirit is love, joy, peace, patience, kindness, goodness, faithfulness, gentleness and self-control. Against such things there is no law" (Galatians 5:22-23 ESV).

The more influence you give the Holy Spirit in your life, the more your character will change; but don't be disappointed when this does not happen all at once. The pattern of spiritual transformation is gradual. The important thing is to view the Holy Spirit as a well and your heart as a container. That is why there are so many phrases in the Bible like "be filled with the Spirit," "receive the Spirit," "be baptized by the Spirit," and "be full of the Spirit." God wants you to get as much of His Spirit as possible.

Tomorrow we will talk more about the Holy Spirit and how He can give us an advantage in life. Until then, continue the journey.

Day 18 Reflection Questions

- Why is it important for you to know who the Holy Spirit is?
- What are some things that the Holy Spirit does for a Christ-follower?
- How can you remain sensitive to the Holy Spirit's voice and guidance?
- In today's reading, Paul says that "God's love has been poured out into our hearts through the Holy Spirit, who has been given to us" (Romans 5:5). How does that change the way you view God's work in your life?

Day 19: God's "X-Factor"

Gatorade knows all about extraordinary. Decades ago, they created a drink called "X-Factor" to give athletes an additional edge. But what makes us extraordinary Christians? Did you know that the Bible teaches us that God has given His children a supernatural "X-Factor"? It is the Holy Spirit, and He enables us to resist the devil and make an extraordinary impact while on earth. Let me explain.

In the very first book of the Bible, we are told that God created us in His image as spiritual beings and said, "Let us make mankind in our image, in our likeness, so that they may rule over the fish in the sea and the birds in the sky, over the livestock and all the wild animals, and over all the creatures that move along the ground" (Genesis 1:26). God created us as spiritual beings to rule over the planet, but Adam and Eve surrendered that authority to the devil when they chose to disobey God and eat the forbidden fruit.

Satan told them that by eating the forbidden fruit, they would become like God and know good and evil. Although Adam and Eve already knew goodness, they had not been exposed to the knowledge of evil. When they disobeyed God and ate the fruit, they were exposed to an evil they could not comprehend or imagine. Their rebellion exposed them to something that permanently tarnished not only their spiritual nature but also everything else around them. It was then that humanity experienced evil and the beginning of our spiritual separation from God.

Because the devil cannot touch God, he continues to focus his attention on destroying God's children. Until we get to heaven, we will continue to exist as spiritual beings fighting against the devil's attempts to destroy God's creation and separate them from God.

That is why God has given us access to supernatural power through the Holy Spirit who helps us recapture some of the spiritual power that was surrendered in the Garden of Eden. Both John the Baptist and Jesus promised that salvation would enable us to access spiritual power for this spiritual battle. That is what John the Baptist meant when he said: "I baptize you with water for repentance. But after me comes one who is more powerful than I, whose sandals I am not worthy to carry. He will baptize you with the Holy Spirit and fire" (Matthew 3:11).

Jesus himself would promise the provision of this spiritual X-Factor when He told His disciples to "wait for the gift my Father promised, which you have heard me speak about. For John baptized with water, but in a few days you will be baptized with the Holy Spirit" (Acts 1:4-5).

Toward the end of Jesus's ministry, He told His disciples that He must return to heaven so they could have access to the Holy Spirit's supernatural power. "I will ask the Father, and he will give you another advocate to help you and be with you forever—the Spirit of truth. The world cannot accept him, because it neither sees him nor knows him. But you know him, for he lives with you and will be in you" (John 14:16-17).

While on earth, Jesus had a limited role inside the context of time and place; but when He returned to His rightful place of authority in heaven, He sent the Holy Spirit to enable the believer to recapture the spiritual power and understanding that was lost in the Garden of Eden.

This promise was finally fulfilled after Jesus ascended into heaven. In Acts 2, the Holy Spirit fell upon the believers and gave them supernatural power and empowered them to be effective witnesses for Christ. Three very important "visible" things happened:

- First, they experienced the sound of wind. Why? Because wind represented the breath of God filling them with His resurrected Spirit.

- Second, they experienced visible tongues of fire that rested over each one of them. Why? Because before Christ, fire was a symbol of God's power and presence; but now the Holy Spirit would enable God's power to rest in the heart of every believer.

- Third, they began to pray in unknown languages as the Spirit of God enabled them. This was to symbolize God's empowering His people with a supernatural form of prayer. It was also a sign to nonbelievers that something divine in nature was happening. A prayer spoken in the native tongue of heaven is like a direct hotline to our heavenly Father.

We see Christ's promise of power poured out over and over again down through the centuries. The Bible teaches us that we can expect the same strength and can continue to be empowered by the Holy Spirit until we get to heaven. So what is the takeaway for you? God has not left you ill-equipped to thrive as a spiritual being nor under resourced. Because you were created as a spiritual being and are part of a cosmic spiritual battle, God has given you access to the tools you will need to be successful on that level.

It is important that you remember you are a spiritual being first and a physical being second. Your physical existence is limited and temporary, but your spiritual existence is eternal. Before you were a Christ-follower, you probably ignored the spiritual side of your existence and focused on the physical, emotional, and mental side; but the Holy Spirit can now bring understanding, purpose, and power to your spiritual existence. The power that Jesus spoke of and promised is a power to help you combat Satan as a spiritual being while here on earth.

The Holy Spirit is the X-Factor that lives within you and empowers you to:

- Be a powerful witness for Christ in this world.
- Live for God with deeper effectiveness and power.
- Confront the spiritual assault that the devil will unleash on this planet.

Just as Jesus provides salvation through His death and resurrection, the Holy Spirit empowers you to draw closer to Jesus and bring others along on the journey.

We will talk more about this tomorrow; but in the meantime, read Romans 6-8. Chapter 8 teaches us how the Holy Spirit helps us pray and gives us supernatural power. Be sure to read it!

Day 19 Reflection Questions

- As a follower of Jesus, what is the nature of the battle in which you find yourself? Why will this battle be fought until Jesus returns?
- As you look at the world around you, where do you see God's will being opposed in tangible ways?
- Why do we need God's own power to keep on fighting and following after Jesus?
- How does God empower us? What are your initial thoughts and feelings about His promise to do that?
- Look at Romans 8:1-11. What does it mean to have life in the Spirit?

Day 20: Is God Still Supernatural?

Welcome to Day 20 of your journey. Today's Bible reading is Romans 9-11.

We are born into a spiritual life whether we realize it or not. God created us in His image so we could interact with Him on a spiritual level. Do you remember how we talked about the fact that God created us with "eternity in our hearts"? Nowhere do we see God's intended purpose for this relationship more clearly than in the Book of Genesis. It is here that we are told that Adam and Eve walked and talked with God in the Garden on a daily basis.

This relationship was hindered and changed when Adam and Eve chose sin over God. However, our sin does not terminate God's desire for relationship. He still desires to share relationship with us and lead us in spiritual things. God bestows spiritual gifts on His children at the moment they return to Him; and these spiritual gifts are listed in 1 Corinthians 12-14, Romans 12, and Ephesians 4. Even though all the gifts are spiritual, I want to divide them into two categories for the sake of simplicity.

The first category is serving gifts. These are spiritual abilities God gives us to serve Him, the Church, and the world. These gifts include abilities like administration, generosity, encouragement, helps, hospitality, leadership, love, and teaching.

The second category is spiritual gifts. These are supernatural abilities God gives us to compete in a supernatural world—gifts like spiritual insight, faith, healing, tongues, interpretation of tongues, knowledge, miracles, prophecy, and wisdom.

On Days 5 and 13, we talked about using our gifts to serve God; but today I would like to speak to you about the purpose and need for the spiritual gifts or, as some call them, "supernatural gifts." As His children, God does not leave us empty-handed or ill-equipped to face the devil's spiritual assaults and manifestations of evil. Spiritual gifts are God's way of giving us the ability to thrive and function in a spiritual world.

A message in tongues followed by an understandable interpretation is God's way of letting us know He wants to lead and direct us into a deeper relationship with Him. Gifts of healing, faith, and miracles have the same purpose as verbal gifts. Each gift should lead believers and unbelievers into a greater awareness of God. Miracles reinforce the gospel's validity and power.

I believe it all goes back to the Garden of Eden where God created us to declare His kingdom to the world. God created each of us to be conduits of His spirituality and power on earth. Once someone realizes the truth of the gospel, they have the opportunity to walk in the power of the Holy Spirit.

Receiving salvation or even being filled with the Spirit does not guarantee a Spirit-empowered life. It is walking in the Spirit daily that keeps us connected to God's supernatural power. That is why there are so many phrases in the Bible like "be filled with the Spirit," "receive the Spirit," "be baptized by the Spirit," and "be full of the Spirit." God wants you to get as much of His Spirit as possible.

The Bible encourages every believer to desire the gifts of the Spirit in their own lives (1 Corinthians 14:1). Believers are strengthened and encouraged by humbly depending upon God and positioning themselves to be used by the Holy Spirit. Our emphasis should not be upon the person who has a gift or even how impressive the gift may be. The believer is just a tool in the hands of the Holy Spirit to advance the kingdom of God and further God's plan of redemption.

In the New Testament, Paul explains the gifts of the Spirit by comparing them to different parts of the body. He does this to communicate how each one of us is gifted to fulfill a unique spiritual role in reaching the world and serving in the community of faith.

People are spiritual and must see their lives through a spiritual lens first and a physical lens second. Since we look through physical eyes at a physical world, we must rely on the Holy Spirit to lead us into spiritual things; and He explains how He will do this by defining the gifts of the Spirit and giving us the example of how others in the Early Church were used by God's Spirit.

You do not need to understand every facet of spiritual gifts right now as much as you need to learn to rely upon God's Spirit to help you live and function in a spiritual world.

Tomorrow we will talk about God's supernatural download—everyone has one, and it is important to recognize it. Until then, continue the journey with the Spirit's help and power.

Day 20 Reflection Questions

- What might keep you from expecting God to work in supernatural ways? Where did those obstacles or hesitations come from?
- Why does God give His people spiritual gifts?
- How does it feel to know that God wants to work in and through you by giving you spiritual gifts?
- Practically speaking, what steps can you take to depend on the Holy Spirit more fully (and more consistently)?
- Turn to the lists of spiritual gifts in Romans 12:6-8 and 1 Corinthians 12:7-11. Have you seen any of these at work in yourself or other believers? Take a moment to pray—asking God to prepare you to use the gifts He gives you!

Day 21: Your Supernatural Download

Today is Day 21 of your journey, and our daily Bible reading is Romans 12-14. In Romans 12 we are told that God has given each one of us something special—a spiritual gift. Let me explain.

We have all downloaded files, music, and movies from the Internet. Well, something similar happened to you the moment you became a new Christian. When you became a Christian, you received a supernatural download from God. The Holy Spirit gave you spiritual gifts to help you make a unique contribution not only to this world but also to God's kingdom. That is what the Bible means when it says: "Now to each one the manifestation of the Spirit is given for the common good" (1 Corinthians 12:7). There are four important things you need to know about these gifts.

First, these gifts are spiritual, not natural. That is why the Bible calls them manifestations of the Spirit or "spiritual gifts." It is important to understand that I am not talking about natural talent or abilities. A spiritual gift is a spiritual ability that has been given to you by God at the time of salvation. The Holy Spirit then empowers you to use that gift to make a unique contribution to the kingdom of God. The Bible lists them in three places: Romans 12:3-9, 1 Corinthians 12-14, and Ephesians 4:7-13. Some examples of these gifts include:

- Prophecy, knowledge, discernment, and wisdom.

- Leadership, administration, and evangelism.
- Pastor, apostle, evangelist, prophet, and teacher.
- Service, mercy, and generosity.
- Faith, healing, and miracles.
- Hospitality, helps, and exhortation.
- Tongues and interpretation of tongues.

These are just a few of the spiritual gifts the Bible mentions.

Be sure to remember that a spiritual gift is not the same as a natural or developed talent. A talent is a capability you were born with or developed. Examples of these abilities include music, athletics, art, or languages. Talents are not spiritual gifts, but they can be platforms that help you use your spiritual gifts. For example, the gift of teaching can be merged with the talent of music to teach music. Isn't it amazing that every child of God has been given a spiritual gift that guarantees them a unique contribution to what God is doing in the world.

Second, spiritual gifts can only be developed in tandem with spiritual maturity. That means developing them requires spiritual growth at the same time. It is possible to have a great talent and still be immature, but it is not possible to possess a highly developed spiritual gift and be spiritually immature. We have all witnessed the disappointing lifestyles of outstanding athletes or celebrities who possess great talent but act like 12-year-olds. Spiritual gifts can only be developed in proportion to your spiritual maturity, and that is why spiritual growth is so important. The more you grow spiritually, the more your spiritual gifts are refined, developed, and matured.

Third, your spiritual gifts reveal God's purpose and plan for your life. Many Christians wonder what God's purpose is for their lives. Sometimes they waste a lot of time and emotional energy trying to discover why God created them, but few things point to your life's purpose more accurately than your spiritual gifts. Why? Because the design of a tool is the best indicator of how that tool should be used. The more you grow and discover your God-given download, the more you will get a glimpse of God's purpose for your life and your unique contribution to the kingdom of God.

Fourth, your church wants to help you discover your spiritual gifts. Once you become more established in your faith, you will want to start exploring God's will in this area; but for now, the most important thing is to focus on learning and applying the teachings of Jesus.

Tomorrow we will talk about why servanthood was so important to Jesus and central to Christian living. We'll talk more then.

Day 21 Reflection Questions

- What is the difference between spiritual gifts and natural abilities? In what ways can the two overlap as you serve God within the local church?
- Why is ongoing spiritual growth so important when it comes to the development and use of these gifts?
- How can you come to a better understanding of God's will for your life by reflecting on the gifts He has given you?

Day 22: Why Serve Others?

Welcome to Day 22. Our daily Bible reading is Romans 15-1 Corinthians 1. You have been a believer for over three weeks now. Congratulations on following Jesus and growing in your faith.

We live in a society where our importance is largely determined by how many people serve us. Our culture tells us that the more successful we become, the more we delegate to others. On the low end, it is having others cut our grass, do our hair, or care for our children. On the higher end, it is about the number of employees, personal assistants, and companies you own. The sky is the limit, right?

What if I were to tell you that Jesus defined His own success and the success of His followers differently? As a matter of fact, He identified service to God and others as the true mark of spiritual maturity. When Jesus was describing His own life's purpose, He said: "The Son of Man did not come to be served, but to serve, and to give his life as a ransom for many" (Matthew 20:28). Paul the apostle acknowledged this when he described how Christ left heaven and put aside His divine power and humbled himself by being a servant (Philippians 2).

You might be wondering why servanthood is so central to the life of Christ and necessary for spiritual growth, so let's talk about why servanthood should be important to a follower of Christ.

The most important reason is that servanthood models the life of Christ. Christ's obedience and humble service to God the Father is our model for Christian service. That is what the Apostle Paul meant when he said our attitude should be the same as that of Christ Jesus, "Who, being in very nature God, did not consider equality with God something to be used to his own advantage; rather, made himself nothing by taking the very nature of a servant, being made in human likeness. And being found in appearance as a man, he humbled himself by becoming obedient to death—even death on a cross!" (Philippians 2:5-8). If we are Christ-followers, then our ultimate goal is to be like Christ. That is why serving God and others helps us be more Christlike and gives us greater purpose in life.

Another reason why service is important is because it is a way we can fulfill our purpose. In Chapter 5, we talked about how God has given each of us a unique set of spiritual gifts to achieve our purpose on earth. That is why the Bible says God wants ALL OF US to be involved in ministry in some way, shape, or form. That does not mean He expects you to quit your job and become a pastor. It means He has given you gifts to serve while you are living out your normal life. God provides pastors to help every believer find a place where they can use their gifts and prepare God's people for works of service (Ephesians 4:12). All of your gifts, natural talents, passions, experiences, and temperament are road signs pointing to a specific way God has empowered you to serve. Once you have identified them and employed your gifts by serving in your sweet spot, you are doing what God placed you on this planet to do. Nothing is as fulfilling as doing what you were born to do!

Are you ready for the third reason to serve? Not only will you better model Christ and fulfill your purpose, but you will also grow spiritually. I know that sounds strange, but one of the most common obstacles to spiritual growth among Christians is that they are not serving. Many are receiving, taking, asking, and consuming resources but never modeling Christ's example of service.

Jesus compared serving to a tree bearing fruit. "I am the vine; you are the branches. If you remain in me and I in you, you will bear much fruit; apart from me you can do nothing . . . This is to my Father's glory, that you bear much fruit, showing yourselves to be my disciples" (John 15:5,8). Wow, that is a challenging statement. Jesus is saying that our fruit is the proof of our discipleship. What is the takeaway? Make sure you are serving in some capacity. That could be in a ministry at your church or volunteering in other ways.

People often ask me the question, "Where should I start serving until I figure some of this stuff out?" I have one favorite suggestion. It is easy, does not require a lot of time, and can help you meet lots of other people in your new church. Every church has a hospitality ministry that serves behind the scenes and is an excellent "on ramp" to service. The hospitality team usually provides ushers and greeters to welcome guests, help people find a seat or a parking spot, and distribute refreshments. It only requires a minimal commitment and is an excellent place to start. If you are interested in learning more, send an email to your pastor or one of the church staff members and ask them to help you find a comfortable place to serve. Why not get started this week?

Find a place to explore your gifts and make a positive contribution to the kingdom.

Day 22 Reflection Questions

- How would our society define success? Does that line up with Jesus's understanding of success?
- Think through the stories you have read of Jesus. Where does He model servanthood? Which ones are your favorites and what can you learn from His example?
- Jesus did not come "to be served, but to serve, and to give his life as a ransom for many" (Matthew 20:28). What does that tell you about His heart and character?
- Why does God want you to serve in and with the local church? What impact will it have on your own life?
- Is there anything holding you back from serving alongside other believers? How can you overcome that?

Day 23: Loving Our World

Today is Day 23 of your new journey, and our daily Bible reading is 1 Corinthians 2-4.

Do you remember a few days ago when we talked about the four basic ingredients of spiritual growth? The first was connecting and worshiping in a community of faith, the second was learning and living God's Word, and the third was serving God and others. The fourth ingredient was loving our world. That is the one ingredient I want to spend a little more time talking to you about today. Some churches refer to loving their world as "outreach." We use that word because its focus is on our reaching out to others rather than reaching in and serving ourselves.

Jesus told the disciples that their impact on the world should start in their own city and expand its influence outward into the entire world. "You will be my witnesses in Jerusalem, and in all Judea and Samaria, and to the ends of the earth" (Acts 1:8). That is why your church seeks to express God's love to the world. It starts:

- Right at home in your immediate neighborhood and community. This might be outreach events to children, teens, the homeless, or the needy in your own city.
- Then it reaches out to assist others who are in need in your state and/or nation. This usually includes supporting workers in drug rehabilitation projects,

church planting where churches do not exist, or regional compassion efforts.

- Finally, we reach out globally through partnerships with missionaries working internationally. This involves many things such as schools overseas, social justice ministries, or helping spread the good news of God's love to the peoples of the world who have no access to Bibles, missionaries, or local churches.

Your church will encourage people to engage themselves on every level. There are lots of ways you can be involved. The important thing is to use your gifts and abilities in some part of the outreach supply chain.

We realize there are opportunities for outreach that present themselves in other areas of our lives; but as a part of God's family, our work will make a greater impact if we partner together. That is what the Bible means when it says: "Two are better than one, because they have a good return for their labor" (Ecclesiastes 4:9).

Following Christ starts with experiencing God through worship and leads into learning and living God's Word. After that, your journey should lead you to serving God and others in the body of Christ. However, sooner or later, you will need to reach out to those in your community and world. It is not only commanded by Christ but also an essential ingredient to your spiritual growth. It may be a single mom in your neighborhood, an elderly person who needs help with yard work, or providing logistical support to a partner organization helping the poor and oppressed. The important thing is to start looking for little ways to reach out to the world around you as you continue the journey.

Day 23 Reflection Questions

- Think about your community, including your workplace and social circles. Who can you impact with the love of Jesus this week?
- How could you help meet some of the needs of your own neighborhood and community at large?
- What is your church already doing that has caught your attention? Would you consider getting involved in that ministry?
- There are so many ways to love the world and opportunities to serve. Why is it important to remain attentive and follow God's guidance when it comes to outreach?
- In today's reading, Paul tells the believers in Corinth that He first came to them in the Spirit's power rather than in His own strength or eloquence (1 Corinthians 2:1-5). What do you think He meant by that?

Day 24: Generosity

It's Day 24 of your new journey. Today our Bible reading is 1 Corinthians 5-7. I want to commend you on allowing the seeds of God's Word to grow in your heart.

I will never forget the day I decided to become a Christ-follower. It was not in an emotionally charged environment with mood music, impressive lighting, and a guilt-ridden message. It was after seeing a slideshow of the crucifixion of Christ. I was a teenager caught in drugs and alcohol and could hardly believe that God gave His one and only Son to restore His relationship with me. The Bible tells us that God loves us so much He cannot help but give. For me, God's love was irresistible.

That is why the Bible says: "For God so loved the world that he gave his one and only son" (John 3:16). Think about that statement, "For God so loved . . . that he gave." Generosity was the natural expression of God's love. True love always gives, releases, and shares. It is just the nature of authentic love. As followers of Christ, this should also be the byproducts of our own relationship with God. Let me explain with a story.

Several years ago when my kids were young, we decided to take a break from our shopping and get a bite to eat in the food court of a local mall. I gave each one of my kids $10 and let them pick which food concession they preferred before meeting at our table to share a meal. My youngest daughter got back first and started eating while I was holding the table and waiting for the others. Watching her eat made me hungry, and I decided to reach out and grab a French fry from her plate. To my surprise, she hovered over those fries with her arms, squinted her eyes, and said, "Hey! Those are mine!" I was a bit surprised. After all, I took $10 out of my own wallet and generously gave it to her so she could buy that meal. Now she somehow forgot all about that and took ownership of what was mine to begin with. I wanted to say, "You don't get it, do you? I bought those fries. I own those fries. As a matter of fact, I have enough resources to bury you in fries if I want to." I still laugh when I think of this story; but wonder if that is how God feels about us at times. He freely shares everything He has with us; but the first time He wants to use us to meet someone else's need, we say, "Hey! That's mine!" But is it?

If God is really at the center of our lives, He should have access not only to our hearts, time, and talents but also to our finances as well; and if He does not have our resources, it is because He does not completely have our hearts. That is what Jesus was talking about when He said: "For where your treasure is, there your heart will be also" (Luke 12:34).

What does generosity have to do with faith anyway? Are they really related? The answer is yes! Our faith should make us want to be generous with the blessings we have received from God. Paul said: "Each of you should give what you have decided in your heart to give, not reluctantly or under compulsion, for God loves a cheerful giver" (2 Corinthians 9:7).

God wants us to use the wealth He gives us on earth to help get more people into heaven. Jesus said, "Do not store up for yourselves treasures on earth, where moths and vermin destroy, and where thieves break in and steal. But store up for yourselves treasures in heaven, where moths and vermin do not destroy, and where thieves do not break in and steal. For where your treasure is, there your heart will be also" (Matthew 6:19-21).

As a matter of fact, Jesus taught us that how we use our money determines the parameter of what we are entrusted with by God. "If you have not been trustworthy in handling worldly wealth, who will trust you with true riches? And if you have not been trustworthy with someone else's property, who will give you property of your own? No one can serve two masters. Either you will hate the one and love the other, or you will be devoted to the one and despise the other. You cannot serve both God and money" (Luke 16:11-13).

We are only on this earth for a short time before spending eternity with God. That is why how we use money and wealth is such an indicator of what God will place in our trust. As a matter of fact, God's Word says that our generosity is actually an expression of our faith. God can and will take care of our needs for "God is able to bless you abundantly, so that in all things at all times, having all that you need, you will abound in every good work" (2 Corinthians 9:8).

Of course, God expects us to take care of our financial obligations and the needs of our family; but in doing so, we are not to neglect our responsibility to give to God's work. If you think about it, everything you know or experienced about God was brought to you on the wings of someone else's generosity. God used the resources of others as a vehicle to reach out to you.

In the Bible this is called a "tithe." Tithe means tenth. The biblical concept of a tithe was a spiritual expression of many things.

- Recognition that everything they had came from God.
- Trust that God would take care of their needs.
- Thankfulness for God's blessings.
- Commitment to the kingdom of God and something bigger than themselves.
- Willingness to obey God.

Someone once told me that the hardest place to let God in is in our wallets. That is why Jesus talked so much about money. He knew that how we spend money is a reflection of our priorities, and getting our priorities straightened out is a good thing. Even if you cannot start giving 10 percent now, start where you can—2 percent or 5 percent—and work up until you reach the tithe.

That is what I did after becoming a Christ-follower. I was only 16 years old and pretty much living on my own. A tithe seemed like a huge amount to me. I had read an Old Testament scripture where God confronted the children of Israel for not having enough faith in Him to tithe and believe He would still take care of their needs. God challenged them saying, "Bring the whole tithe into the storehouse, that there may be food in my house. Test me in this, . . . and see if I will not throw open the floodgates of heaven and pour out so much blessing that there will not be room enough to store it" (Malachi 3:10). I realized I had more faith to believe that

God could save me from my sins than He could meet my financial needs if I tithed. My budget was tight, but I decided to take God up on the challenge and "test" Him by slowly wading into the waters of tithing with a four-stage plan to get me tithing in four months.

- **Stage 1 involved taking a step of obedience.** The Bible says to "honor the LORD with your wealth, with the firstfruits" (Proverbs 3:9). So my first step was deciding to believe this scripture and obey God by writing a check for 2.5 percent (one quarter of my tithe) of my total income.

- **Stage 2 involved taking a step of sacrifice.** When deciding to make a financial contribution to God's work, King David said, "I will not sacrifice to the LORD my God burnt offerings that cost me nothing" (2 Samuel 24:24). I decided to do the same and looked over my monthly expenses and cut things out of my budget that I could do without. I cut out enough things to total what would be another 2.5 percent (another one quarter of my tithe) of my total income. This encouraged me because with very little effort, I was up to 5 percent (one half of my tithe) of my total income in two months.

- **Stage 3 involved taking a step of faith.** "Faith is confidence in what we hope for and assurance about what we do not see" (Hebrews 11:1). I then increased my tithe to 7.5 percent believing that God would miraculously provide the increase from 5 percent to 7.5 percent. You know what? He did! I received a rebate in the mail, an unexpected gift, a refund, a gift card, and a discount on something I had planned on purchasing. After three months, I was now tithing 7.5 percent of my total income.

- **Stage 4 involved taking a step of thanksgiving.** I noticed that the Bible records God's people giving thank offerings to the Lord: "Let them sacrifice thank offerings and tell of his works with songs of joy" (Psalm 107:22). God's people would often give a financial offering of thankfulness if they returned safely from a long and treacherous trip, if they were healed of a disease, or if they experienced God's miraculous provision. It dawned on me that I had much to be thankful to God for and decided to give an additional 2.5 percent as an expression of gratitude to God.

In four months, I had grown my faith and my tithe into 10 percent of my income and have not stopped since. As a matter of fact, several years ago, I stopped keeping track and am blown away every year when I do my taxes and discover that my wife and I have been able to give 20 percent without noticing it. To be honest, it has become a fun and fulfilling expression of obedience and faith.

Why not start investing in the kingdom of God now so others might know and experience what you know. Try trusting God with what He has entrusted to you. You will not regret it.

Tomorrow we are going to talk about what to do when you have tough questions about faith, but I want to give you a challenge this week. Try being generous with your finances and see how you feel after a week. Wade into the waters of financial obedience and see if you feel better or worse. See if your needs are still met. I did, and I have not stopped since.

Day 24 Reflection Questions

- In your own words, what does it mean to be generous? Have you ever seen or benefited from that?
- How does the arrival and death of Jesus demonstrate the generosity of God?
- Why does God expect His people to be generous with their love, forgiveness, time, talent, and resources?
- What are your initial thoughts about giving part of your income back to God? Willingness, hesitation? Why?
- Jesus said, "For where your treasure is, there your heart will be also" (Luke 12:34). How does your wallet reveal your priorities?

Day 25: Doubt and Tough Questions of Faith

Welcome to Day 25 of your journey. Today's Bible reading is 1 Corinthians 8-10.

We read how the Apostle Paul addressed some of the difficult questions early believers had about faith, controversial subjects, and day-to-day living. Sooner or later all Christians face doubt about their faith whether it is being challenged by people from other faiths, facing tragedy, or being let down by other believers. Today I want to address this important issue by giving you three encouraging facts about doubt and questions of faith.

The first thing I want you to understand is that it is not a sin to ask tough questions about faith. It is normal and certainly not a sin to ask questions that verge on doubt. When God asks us to put our faith in Him, He is not asking us to believe without proof, reasons, or evidence. Faith in God is to believe that He is who He says He is and that He will do what He says He will do. It is only when we are doubting God's character or Word that we sin.

Doubting the completeness of our understanding of the facts is never a sin. God requires us to have knowing faith because He Himself provides evidence. Christians believe what they do because of facts, not in spite of them. Many times God says "test Me," or "prove Me." Not only is it not a sin to test our beliefs, our faith, or even the existence of God or the Bible as His Word, but I also believe it would be a sin for us not to do so. Science is not the adversary of God as some believe. Instead, the belief in the God of the Bible and His order in His creation is what enabled and launched what we call modern science.

Since the time of Galileo, people have wrongly thought that science and faith exist in contradiction to each other. However, the facts of science only confirm the truth of God and His Word. It is only the misinterpretation of those facts that are at odds with God. For example, consider Charles Darwin who is credited by many as the man who developed a theory which made faith in the first 11 chapters of Genesis unnecessary. If Darwin knew then what science knows today, according to his own words, he would willingly abandon the theory and indeed the religion of evolution. He claimed that if certain things were known and shown, his theory would collapse and be of no account. Those very things are now known to be true. It is only through a willing rejection of God's truth that the evolutionary worldview persists today.

We serve a God who is both Light and Truth. Truth does not fear the light; and as Christians, we do not flinch from scrutiny or questions. As we follow the Truth, the brighter the light and the more piercing the questions, the more our faith is vindicated and established.

The second thing I want you to understand is that there are even biblical examples of godly people who asked God tough questions. Moses, Daniel, David, Job, Paul, Jeremiah, and many others asked hard questions of God. God did not object to the questions at all when they were asked in all earnestness. Indeed, He provided answers and

110

encouraged questions and scrutiny as God does not want us to have blind faith. He wants us to know and trust Him. We cannot do either without reason. God knows this and does not require us to do so.

The third thing I want you to understand is that how we process doubt is more important than the existence of doubt itself. Whether we are in a time of crisis, tragedy, or the apparent presence of chaos, it is how we process doubt that is important. How do we do that? Allow me to make a few suggestions.

It is important to try and determine the source of your doubt. Is it because something bad happened? Is it because someone else from a different faith seems more passionate about their beliefs than you? Is it because God seems far away? You need to find out why you are doubting so you can face those circumstances head-on.

It also helps to pray about your doubt. God is secure enough to handle your being open and transparent with your doubts. That's what happened when a man in need confessed to Jesus: "I do believe; help me overcome my unbelief!" (Mark 9:24). Let God know what you are facing and ask Him to strengthen your faith. In the shadow of doubt, it may feel like God is far away; but He is not—He is listening.

Staying in the Word is also critical. God's Spirit will help you see and understand things in the Bible that speak directly to your situation; but if you let discouragement lead you away from God's Word, you will never find answers.

Talking to someone about your doubt is also helpful. Some Christians don't talk to others about their doubts because they think they will be judged, but talking with a more mature believer will help you. They can talk to you about your doubts, share their own experiences, and help you continue to grow in your faith.

Lastly, take advantage of Christian resources. There are numerous great resources that can help you. Let me suggest two. The first is the Christian Apologetics and Research Ministry (www.carm.org). The second is a book entitled *The New Evidence That Demands a Verdict* by Josh McDowell. As Christians in this modern information age, we are surrounded by more helpful resources than at any other time in human history.

Even as science develops a better and more complete understanding of the universe, God and His Word are being vindicated and authenticated more completely and more clearly than ever before.

Tomorrow we will look at what the Bible has to say about prophecy and how the world will end. Until then, continue the journey.

Day 25 Reflection Questions

- Have you faced any doubts since deciding to follow Jesus? If so, how have you handled them thus far?
- Is faith the same thing as blind trust? Explain.
- Why should Christians not be afraid of the search for truth? How does that change your perspective on questions and scrutiny?

- What should you do when doubts arise? Who could you ask to join you in that process?
- In the past few weeks, you have been reading God's Word and responding in prayer. How has He used this to give you greater confidence or increase your faith?

Day 26: How Will It All End?

Welcome to Day 26. Our daily Bible reading is 1 Corinthians 11-13.

In 1 Corinthians 13:12, Paul compared our present understanding of the future to a cloudy reflection, but he reassures us with the fact that one day our understanding of God will be as clear as seeing Christ "face-to-face."

Scriptural references to God's plans for the future that have yet to come is called prophecy. Understanding Bible prophecy can be difficult because some prophecies were intended to be interpreted literally while others were meant to be symbolic. For example, the prophecy that Jesus was to be born in Bethlehem was obviously intended to be taken literally; but when Revelation 6:13 says the "stars in the sky fell to earth", it is a symbolic reference. That's why it is important to interpret prophecy in its intended context, especially the biblical prophecies about how the world will end.

To give you a "big picture" view of prophecy describing the end-times, I am going to do two things. First, I am going to introduce you to the most common terms in biblical prophecy; and then I am going to put them together as I understand God's Word to give you a bird's-eye view.

Let's start by introducing you to the most common phrases in biblical prophecy. Even though views may vary on how these phrases or events fit together, there is nearly 100 percent agreement concerning their validity among those who believe the Bible to be the inspired Word of God. Let's look at the ten most common phrases in biblical prophecy:

"The Second Coming" is a phrase that refers to the return of Jesus Christ to earth at an unknown time in the future. Jesus promised us He would return: "If I go and prepare a place for you, I will come back and take you to be with me that you also may be where I am" (John 14:3). Unfortunately, every five to seven years, some well-intentioned "rocket scientist" claims to have figured out the exact date that Christ will return; but when speaking of His own return, Jesus said, "About that day or hour no one knows, not even the angels in heaven, nor the Son, but only the Father" (Matthew 24:36). Jesus repeats this statement and adds: "Be on guard! Be alert! You do not know when that time will come" (Mark 13:33). That is why it is better to spend more time and energy in being ready for Christ's return than in trying to predict it.

"The Rapture" is the sudden and miraculous departure of all Christians from the earth to meet Christ in the air. The Apostle Paul taught this very specifically when he said: "For the Lord himself will come down from heaven, with a loud command, with the voice of the archangel and with the trumpet call of God, and the dead in Christ will rise first. After that, we who are still alive and are left will be caught up together with them in the clouds to meet the Lord in the air" (1 Thessalonians 4:16-17).

"The Millennial Reign" refers to a thousand-year period of time in the future when Christ reigns on the earth. Its name comes from the word millennium which means 1,000 in Latin. Revelation 20 speaks about this.

"The Great Tribulation" is a seven-year period of world-wide hardships, disasters, famine, war, and suffering on the earth. This time was first mentioned by Jesus in Mark 13:19 and is referenced again in Revelation 2 and 7.

"The Antichrist" will be Satan's key agent on earth who will embody evil, persecute believers, and unify non-believers in a global resistance to God during the end-times. He is described in 1 John 2:18-22.

"Armageddon" is the last and final battle between good and evil before the Day of Judgment (Revelation 16:16).

"The Judgment Seat of Christ" is the place where all Christians will receive their reward for the quality of their life and work on earth. The Apostle Paul said: "For we must all appear before the judgment seat of Christ, so that each of us may receive what is due us for the things done while in the body, whether good or bad" (2 Corinthians 5:10).

"The Great White Throne Judgment" is a place where everyone who has rejected God will experience the eternal consequences of unbelief. Revelation 20:11-14 speaks about this.

"Heaven" is the ultimate and eternal destination of every living person who has believed in God and committed their lives to Christ. Jesus spoke about this in John 14:6, and Revelation 7:13-17 describes it.

"Hell" is the ultimate and eternal destination of every living person who has rejected God and His offer of mercy, grace, and forgiveness found in Christ. Jesus spoke of hell in Matthew 10:28, and Revelation 20:11-15 describes it.

Now let's talk about how all these things fit together. As I understand Scripture, the rapture of the church will take place first, followed by the Great Tribulation. The Antichrist will orchestrate an international coalition to gather the armies of this world in rebellion against God at Armageddon. Then Christ will return with believers and the host of heaven at the battle of Armageddon. This will be followed by the millennial reign of Christ. Then the final judgment of nonbelievers will occur followed by eternity for believers in heaven and nonbelievers in hell.

It is easy to lose sight of the most important lessons from Bible prophecy. The takeaway is not found in arguing about mysterious gray areas but in knowing there is a certainty to God's reign, our eternal hope, and the total defeat of evil.

Tomorrow we will talk more about heaven and hell. Until then, stay current on your Bible reading.

Day 26 Reflection Questions

- Scripture clearly teaches that God knows all things and chooses to reveal whatever He wishes to mankind. How does that inform your understanding of prophecy?
- The biblical narrative begins and ends with God's desire to dwell among humanity in a world unbroken by sin. What does that tell you about His plans or your own purpose?
- How might an expectation of the Second Coming affect the way you live?
- Why is it important to know, even now, that the purposes of God prevail in the end?

Day 27: Heaven and Hell — Location, Location, Location!

Welcome to Day 27. Today's Bible reading is 1 Corinthians 14-16.

Yesterday we talked about biblical prophecy. Today's reading in 1 Corinthians 15 speaks about when our bodies will be resurrected to spend eternity with Christ. That leads right into a brief summary of heaven and hell. Let's talk about hell first.

"Hell" is the ultimate and eternal destination of every living person who rejects God and His plan of redemptive salvation. Jesus spoke of hell in Matthew 10:28, and Revelation 20:11-15 describes it. Hell can be a tough subject to swallow. To some, it may seem unfair or inconsistent with the nature of a loving God; but there are two things we need to remember. One is that the Bible very clearly teaches us that hell is a real place. Second, it is important to remember that God's sense of justice is far more developed than our own. The Bible encourages us to remember that "my thoughts are not your thoughts, neither are your ways my ways, declares the LORD. As the heavens are higher than the earth, so are my ways higher than your ways and my thoughts than your thoughts" (Isaiah 55:8-9).

Our challenge is discovering what the Bible says about hell rather than to trying to build upon our own preferences or limited understanding of God and the universe. Biblical scholars are in disagreement as to whether the Bible's description of hell's suffering is literal in a physical sense or metaphorical in a spiritual sense. In other words, it is unclear whether a person in hell will experience eternal fire and never be consumed or if the imagery of eternal fire is meant to symbolize the eternal suffering in a spiritual or mental sense from being separated from God. In my opinion, it really does not matter. Why? Because both sides of the debate agree the Bible teaches that hell is a place of endless suffering. Whether that suffering is physical or spiritual is somewhat overshadowed by the fact that it is eternal—as in FOREVER!

We must remember that hell is the consequence of rejecting the character, love, and spiritual redemption of our Creator. In my mind, the existence of hell is not inconsistent with a loving God. The idea that "a God of love would never send a soul to hell" can only be supported if it is conveniently isolated from everything else that God has done to save us from hell. Our God has made a way for every one of us to escape the torment of hell. A loving God sent His Son to pay the price for our sins and to make the existence of hell irrelevant for those who choose to believe. That love does not just save us FROM something but also saves us TO something; namely, heaven.

"Heaven" is the ultimate and eternal destination of every living person who believes in God and commits their life to Christ. Jesus spoke about this in John 14:6, and Revelation 7:13-17 describes it. The Bible gives us many specific Scriptures that describe heaven. To begin with, it is a real place. Since the Bible teaches us that we will have resurrected bodies, it would seem reasonable to conclude that heaven is a place where our physical bodies can function in a physical existence.

Heaven is also a beautiful place. The Bible describes it as a city of immense size. Author Max Anders in his book entitled, *Everything Believers Need to Know*, reminds us about that historic picture of the astronauts orbiting the planet with the earth looking like a beautiful marble hanging in space 200 miles behind them. However, the Bible's description of heaven makes earth look like a garbage dump. Revelation 21:16 describes heaven as a city that is fifteen hundred miles long and wide. That is seven times higher than the astronauts' orbit! But size is not the only thing that is impressive about heaven. The Bible describes it as having streets of gold, walls made from precious jewels, and gates of pearl. Heaven is a place where "God will wipe away all tears from their eyes; and there shall be no more death, neither sorrow, nor crying, neither shall there be any more pain: for the former things have passed away" (Revelation 21:4 Webster's Bible Translation). It is a place where millions upon millions will be worshiping God. The Bible also says we will have glorified bodies in heaven.

However, these things in and of themselves are not the most valuable assets of heaven. Our greatest asset is hope—hope that the greatest longing of our hearts will be fulfilled, justice will prevail, and that we will live with God forever!

That is why you need to continue your journey and finish this race of faith so we can be together in heaven instead of the other option God has worked so hard for us to avoid.

Day 27 Reflection Questions

- What was your understanding of heaven and hell prior to this chapter? How has that changed?
- Why do we sometimes find the concept of judgment and hell difficult? How do we reconcile it with what we know of God's love, holiness, and justice?
- Does the reality of hell change your perspective about the importance of telling others the good news about Jesus? Why or why not?
- While reading the description of life in heaven, what stood out to you the most?
- As you read 1 Corinthians 15, where do you see reasons for hope and joy in Jesus Christ?

Day 28: Baptism — Why It's Important

Today is Day 28 of your journey, and our daily Bible reading is 2 Corinthians 1-3.

By now you have probably noticed a pattern of water baptism in your Bible reading. Why did Jesus command His followers to be baptized? Is it really important? Baptism is to the believer what a wedding ring is to a married couple—an outward symbol of that person's total commitment to another.

Unfortunately, the practice and meaning of baptism is slowly losing its significance in contemporary Christianity. To help you understand why it was so important to Jesus, let me take the wedding ring analogy a bit further.

To the best of our knowledge, the Egyptians were the first to use the wedding ring. Because its circle did not have a beginning or an end, it was a popular symbol for eternity. The hole in the middle symbolized a doorway or passage to happiness. Over time, the ring began to be associated with the never-ending love and commitment between two married people. It was worn on the third finger of the left hand because it was believed that the vein in that finger was directly connected to the heart. Eventually the rings were made out of metal and began to be considered a legally binding commitment between a husband and a wife. The ring was an outward expression of an inner reality.

When a person wears a wedding ring today, they are doing two things: making a personal commitment to the one they love and making a public commitment that they belong to someone. That is what baptism is—a symbol of your personal commitment to follow Christ and a public commitment to others that you are not ashamed to be identified with Jesus. It is your way of saying that your love for Christ is not a fleeting emotion but comes straight from the center of your heart.

That is why baptism was and is important to God. That is why Jesus instructed His followers to be baptized: "Therefore go and make disciples of all nations, baptizing them in the name of the Father and of the Son and of the Holy Spirit, and teaching them to obey everything I have commanded you" (Matthew 28:19-20).

What are you saying by wearing the ring of baptism? You are essentially saying four important things:

Baptism is a sign that you are united with Jesus. When you are baptized as a Christ-follower, people understand that you are identifying yourself with Jesus. Baptism is symbolic of your identification with Christ in His burial and resurrection. When the person being baptized is lowered under the water, it signifies their identification with Christ's dying for their sins. Coming up out of the water identifies with His resurrection to newness of life. "Having been buried with him in baptism, in which you were also raised with him through your faith in the working of God, who raised him from the dead" (Colossians 2:12).

Baptism is a sign that your sins have been washed away. The water used in baptism is a symbol of Christ's

124

cleansing us from our sin. That is why three days after Paul became a Christian, a disciple named Ananias came to him and said: "Now what are you waiting for? Get up, be baptized and wash your sins away, calling on his name" (Acts 22:16). That is why in every instance in the Bible where a baptism takes place, the person was immersed in water. Your own baptism will be a powerful declaration that you have accepted the fact that Jesus has forgiven your sins.

The practice of sprinkling for baptism came about after Christianity became the official religion of the Roman Empire under Constantine. Under his edict, entire communities needed to be baptized; and it was simpler and faster to sprinkle large crowds than baptize people individually.

Baptism is a sign of your commitment to be a Christ-follower. In biblical times, it was common for people to be baptized soon after their decision to follow Christ. "Those who accepted his message were baptized, and about three thousand were added to their number that day" (Acts 2:41). Baptism is still a powerful expression of obedience and a willingness to follow Christ. It is your way of telling the world that Christ is now the leader and master of your present and future. It is your way of saying, "My life is under new management. God is the Lord, Savior, and leader of my life."

Baptism is an opportunity for others to hear about God's love. It is common for people in our culture to make public announcements about important things in their lives. People put political signs in their yards to let others know how they intend to vote. Parents put bumper stickers on their cars to let everyone know their kids made the honor role. Young couples make pregnancy announcements and gender reveals to let their friends know a baby is on the way. Baptism is another form of a "good news" announcement we communicate to others. It is a symbolic message of our priorities and life change.

As a matter of fact, when someone was baptized in the times of Christ, it was at the local river and witnessed by family, friends, and members of their local community. Strangely enough, there is not one private baptism recorded in the New Testament. That does not mean that private baptisms are less legitimate but that water baptism for the Early Church was a public declaration of faith. "The whole Judean countryside and all the people of Jerusalem went out to him. Confessing their sins, they were baptized by him in the Jordan River" (Mark 1:5). It is still common today for family and friends to support a person by attending their baptism. Even though they may not have personally made a commitment to follow Christ, they are able to be encouraged by that person's decision.

At this point, allow me to address some of the most common questions about baptism:

- **Why do many churches not baptize children or infants?** There are two primary reasons why most churches do not baptize infants. One is that nowhere in the Bible (Old or New Testaments) do we find an example of children being baptized. We find examples of children being dedicated to the Lord by their parents but not baptized in or sprinkled with water. The second reason is that baptism is a reflection of a conscious decision. It requires a person to have made a deliberate resolution to accept Jesus Christ as their personal Savior. Infants are not capable of making that kind of decision. Most churches rely upon the judgment of parents in deciding when a child is ready to be baptized.

- **What if I have been baptized before?** Many people who may have drifted from their faith and later reached a point of recommitment desire to be baptized again as a testimony to their renewed commitment. Although the Bible only requires one baptism, it does not restrict a person from being baptized more than once.

- **Does baptism assure me that I will go to heaven?** No, it does not. Baptism does not produce salvation but is a product of salvation.

- **Does baptism require church membership or make me a church member?** In most cases, you do not have to become a member of a church to be baptized; and being baptized in water does not automatically make you a member of a church. Baptism is a step of obedience to the teachings of Jesus; membership is a commitment of community you make to others.

Scripture indicates that the only requirement for baptism is that a person experience salvation by accepting Jesus Christ into their life and committing to an ongoing spiritual relationship with Him. That is why I would encourage you to seriously consider being baptized. If you would like to explore the possibility, your church can provide you with additional information about how and when they hold baptismal services. You need only make a phone call or send an email to your pastor to learn how.

Tomorrow we will talk about Communion and how it relates to us today. Until then, I want to commend you for taking the time to invest in your faith and encourage you to continue the journey.

Day 28 Reflection Questions

- Does baptism in water literally wash you clean or save you from sin? Explain.
- How does baptism demonstrate someone's identification with Jesus and His people?
- What makes the act of being baptized a serious decision? Why is it so life changing, both here and in nations where the gospel is suppressed or forbidden?
- Why should baptism be done in public if at all possible?
- If you have not been baptized since deciding to follow Jesus, reach out to someone in your church who could help you take that next step!

Day 29: Communion — The Flag of Our Faith

Welcome to Day 29. Our daily Bible reading is 2 Corinthians 4-6.

How are you doing with your Bible reading? If you have fallen behind, don't get overwhelmed with guilt or try to make up missed reading. Just jump back into the schedule where you should be today and get back on track. If you are keeping pace, great job! Keep it up.

Did you know how "The Star Spangled Banner" was written? Francis Scott Key was an American prisoner on an enemy warship who watched anxiously as the British hurled cannon fire at Fort McHenry (Baltimore, Maryland). All that day and through the night, Key could hear the sounds of the massive assault upon the fort. At dawn, the outcome was still uncertain. Then at 7 a.m., a rocket's blast of light revealed a clear view through the smoke. Key was filled with joy as he saw the red, white, and blue of the American flag still flying high and triumphant over the walls of Fort McHenry.

Key pulled an unfinished letter from his pocket and penned the words of "The Star Spangled Banner":

Oh, say can you see, by the dawn's early light, what so proudly we hailed at the twilight's last gleaming? Whose broad stripes and bright stars, thro' the perilous fight, o'er the ramparts we watched, were so gallantly streaming? And the rockets' red glare, the bombs bursting in air, gave proof thro' the night that our flag was still there. Oh, say does that star-spangled banner yet wave, o'er the land of the free, and the home of the brave?"

Just as the American flag is a symbol of the ideals of this nation so is Communion a powerful symbol of Christ's accomplishment on the cross. In a sense, Communion is the flag of our faith and the anthem of a free people! That is why Jesus told us to continue celebrating it until He returns.

Today Christians from all over the globe partake of Communion in small informal gatherings and large group events. Different churches call it by different names. Some refer to it as Communion and others as the Lord's Table while liturgical churches call it the Eucharistand and some the Lord's Supper. You may have even heard it called the "Passover," and that is because Jesus chose to have the first Communion celebration with His disciples during the Jewish celebration of Passover. The Passover was the Jewish commemoration of the time when God delivered the Israelites from Egypt. God did this by allowing the angel of death to "pass over" every Jewish house that had the blood of a lamb painted on the sides and tops of the doorframes (Exodus 12:7). When Jesus initiated the first Communion celebration during Passover and commanded that it be repeated, He was reminding us that He is the perfect Lamb of God that was sacrificed for us and now protects us from sin's shadow of death.

No matter what it may be called, there are two common denominators:

- Bread is used to remind us that Jesus's body was broken or sacrificed for our sins.
- A cup of juice is used to symbolize Jesus's blood that was shed for our redemption.

The Apostle Paul warned New Testament believers about becoming desensitized to Communion (1 Corinthians 11:23-28). Why is Communion still important to us today, and what should you get out of it? Let me mention three things.

First, Communion should be a time of remembrance. Jesus said: "This cup is the new covenant in my blood; do this, whenever you drink it, in remembrance of me" (1 Corinthians 11:25). When you take Communion, you should remember the sinless life and atoning death of Christ who "bore our sins in his own body on the cross, so that we might die to sins and live for righteousness; by his wounds you have been healed" (1 Peter 2:24). In one grand display of love, God's Son became the canvas of every sin the world has ever committed in the past, present, and future. Like a sponge, Christ absorbed every sin of dishonesty, lust, adultery, pornography, deceit, murder, and every other vice you can think of.

Second, Communion should be a time of proclamation. Whether you realize it or not, every time you take Communion, you are preaching your own sermon: "For whenever you eat this bread and drink this cup, you proclaim the Lord's death until He comes" (1 Corinthians 11:26). The word "proclaim" means to announce, declare, or broadcast. Every time we partake of the Lord's Supper, we are showing the world:

- That Christ is our Savior.
- That we have been forgiven of our sins.
- That we are united with Christ.
- That He is returning for us.

The Lord's Supper is an expression of hope and anticipation that God has not left us as orphans but is coming back for us. It is a bold and righteous declaration that all of history is moving toward a victorious triumph.

Third, Communion should be a time of reflection. "So then, whoever eats the bread or drinks the cup of the Lord in an unworthy manner will be guilty of sinning against the body and blood of the Lord. Everyone ought to examine themselves before they eat of the bread and drink from the cup" (1 Corinthians 11:27-28). Every time you take Communion, you should stand in the shadow of the cross and have the courage to ask yourself a few tough questions:

- Am I honoring God with my decisions and values?
- Do I need God's forgiveness?
- How should I act because I am forgiven?

You might have noticed that the American flag looks like it is placed on backwards on the sleeves of our soldiers. There is a reason for that. The flag patch is sown on with the blue facing forward just like it would be if it were flying in the wind and leading them to a victorious battle. In the same way, Communion should be our way of symbolizing Christ's atonement that goes before us in all we do!

So the next time Communion is celebrated at church or in your small group, honor God by being there. Remember His sacrifice, proclaim your eternal hope, and be sure to ask yourself tough questions as you stand in the shadow of the cross.

We will talk more tomorrow about exactly what it means to make Christ the "Lord" of your life.

Day 29 Reflection Questions

- How does Communion symbolize Jesus's sacrifice on the cross? From where does this tradition come?
- Why do we still observe Communion? What impact will it have on your own life?
- Why is the taking of Communion a perfect moment to reflect on your walk with Jesus and His work for you?
- Summarize the significance of Communion in your own words.
- Today you read that God "made him to be sin who knew no sin, so that in him we might become the righteousness of God" (2 Corinthians 5:21). As you think about that incredible sacrifice which is symbolized in Communion, how does it make you feel?

Day 30: Lordship — Faith Is Not a Hobby

Welcome to Day 30. Today our Bible reading is 2 Corinthians 7-9.

It has been a month since your decision to follow Christ, and you have come so far. I want to congratulate you for the commitment you have shown in following Christ this past month. You have established a daily habit for reading your Bible. You have learned so much about God, His love, and His unbelievable plan for your life. In short, you have established the kind of spiritual disciplines that will keep your faith vibrant and strong. You have become a disciple of Christ.

I want to close this book by speaking with you about living your life with Christ as more than Savior. I want to talk to you about what the Bible calls "lordship." Being an authentic Christ-follower is much, much more than a weekend hobby. It involves followership, obedience, and friendship. Let me explain.

When Jesus called His first disciples, the command was simple. He said: "Follow me!" So the first characteristic of a disciple is one who leaves what they have been doing and follows Jesus wherever He leads, but being a disciple goes beyond simple following. It involves being consistent in allowing the teachings of Christ to shape your values, priorities, and behaviors. Jesus said: "Whoever has my commands and keeps them is the one who loves me. The one who loves me will be loved by my Father, and I too will love them and show myself to them" (John 14:21).

Following Christ is a lot like an iceberg. In the beginning, we willingly surrender everything we know to Him; but as time goes on and the tip of previously surrendered parts of our lives begins to melt off, more rises out of the water and is exposed. Your challenge will be to continue to trust God as more of the parts of your life that have not been surrendered begin to be exposed to His love and grace.

Many people claim to believe in Jesus but have no intention of obeying Him when it is inconvenient or in conflict with their own will. They have a kind of affection for Jesus but never make Him Lord of everything. For them, Christianity is a hobby—not a lifestyle.

We see this shift in the New Testament when the disciples stopped calling Jesus "teacher" and started calling Him "Lord." In the times of Christ, the word "Lord" meant "owner," "master," or "the one to whom I belong." It is not until we follow Christ as Lord that we really get to know Him personally. It was at this level of commitment that Jesus said to His disciples: "I no longer call you servants, because a servant does not know his master's business. Instead, I have called you friends, for everything that I learned from my Father I have made known to you" (John 15:15). That is what I want your relationship with God to grow into—a friendship.

In closing, I need to share something with you. I must tell you how excited I am that you finished this journey! I am so grateful and even humbled that you have trusted me with your time reading this book. You have surrendered more and more of your life to God each and every day. This is only the beginning, and God has wonderful things planned for your future. I am reminded of Jeremiah 29:11: "'For I know the plans I have for you,' declares the LORD, 'plans to prosper you and not to harm you, plans to give you hope and a future.'"

However, I need you to understand something—your church and pastor are there for you! I mean that! If you need any help getting settled into your new church family or have any questions, you know where to find them. They are just a call or email away. Take care and finish strong.

Day 30 Reflection Questions

- What has God done in, for, or through you this month? Give Him thanks for that and share it with others!
- Why must we see faith in Jesus as more than a hobby that we practice on Sunday morning? What is it really?
- What are some practical examples of how following Jesus changes your everyday life?
- You have now spent 30 days listening to God by reading His Word! How will you continue to make this habit part of your daily routine?
- Why is it so necessary to continue your journey with Jesus in a supportive community of believers (a local church)?

Made in United States
North Haven, CT
12 April 2023